Snowmen Hello Winter Coloring Book For Kids

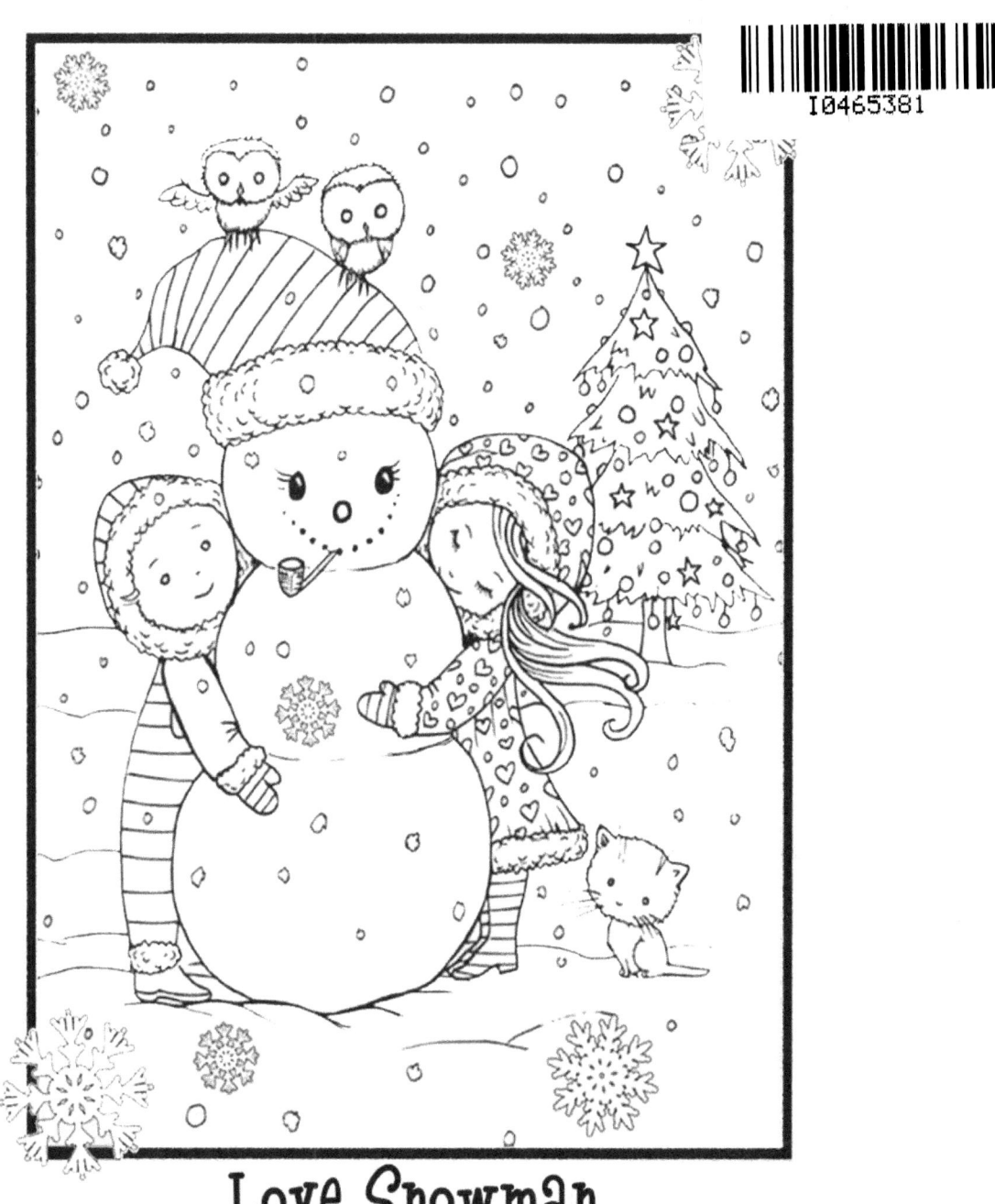

Love Snowman

Nina Watson

Snowmen Hello Winter Coloring Book For Kids and Family

Copyright: Published in the United States by **Nina Watsson**
Published November 2017

ISBN-13: 978-1981184576

ISBN-10: 1981184570

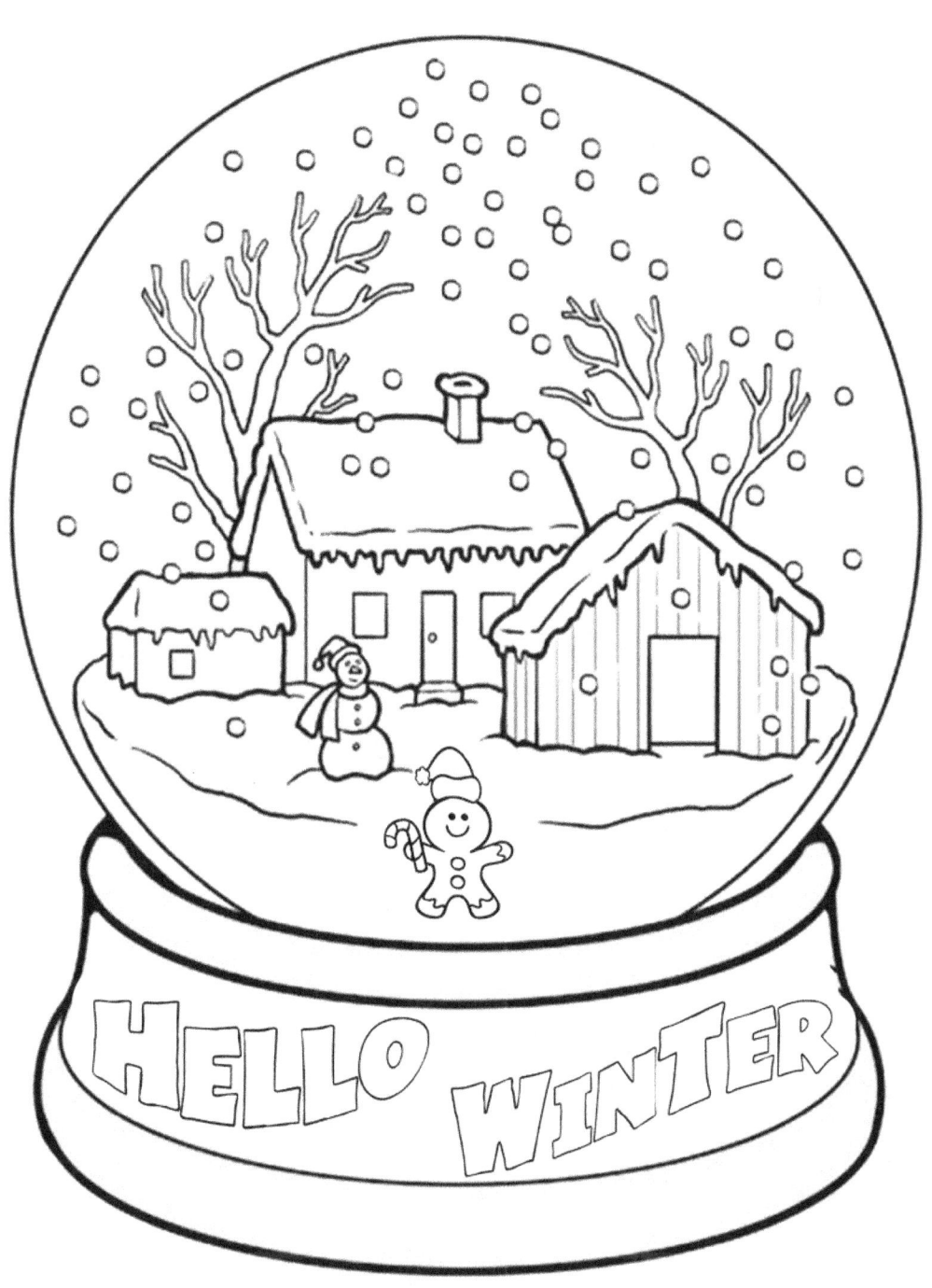

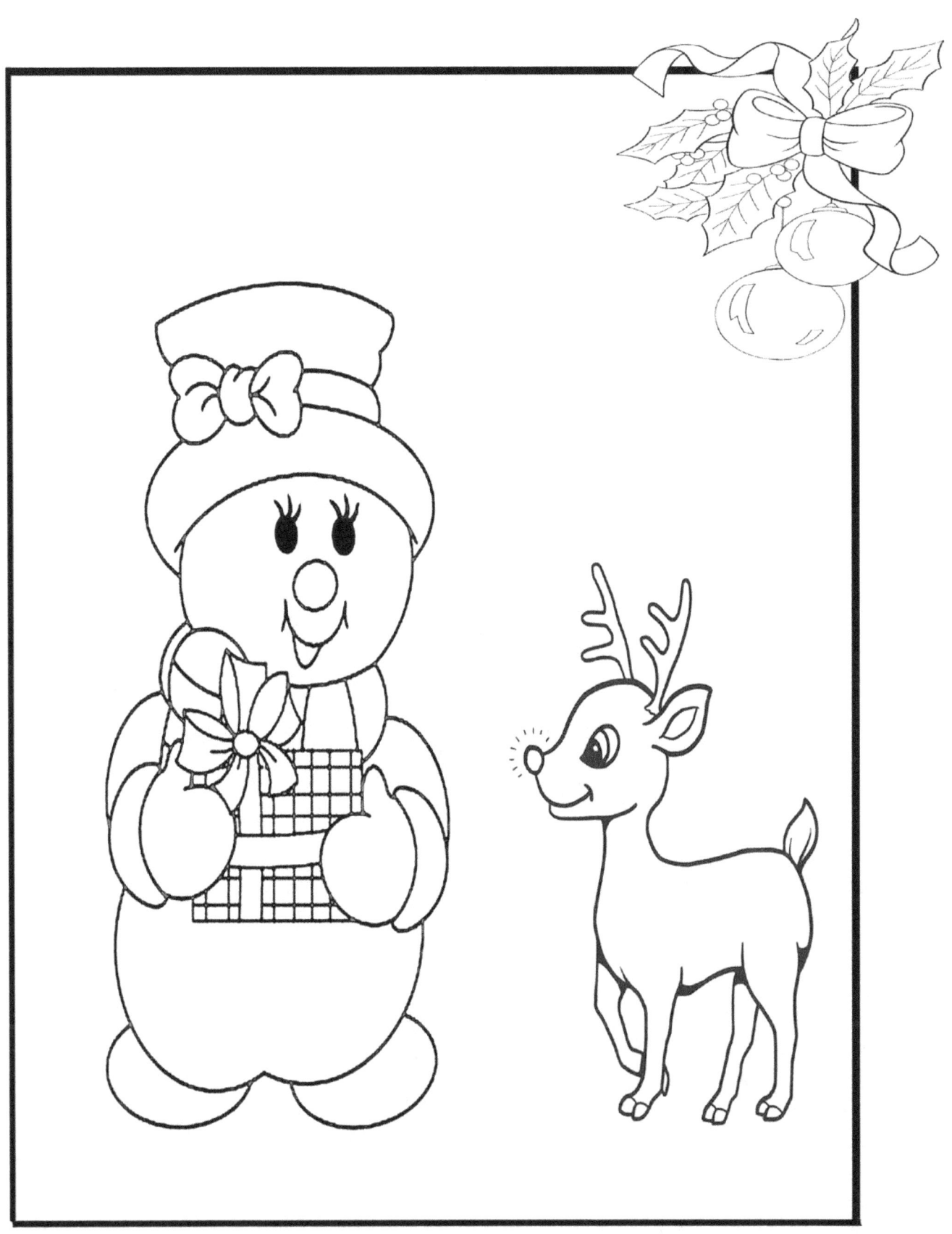

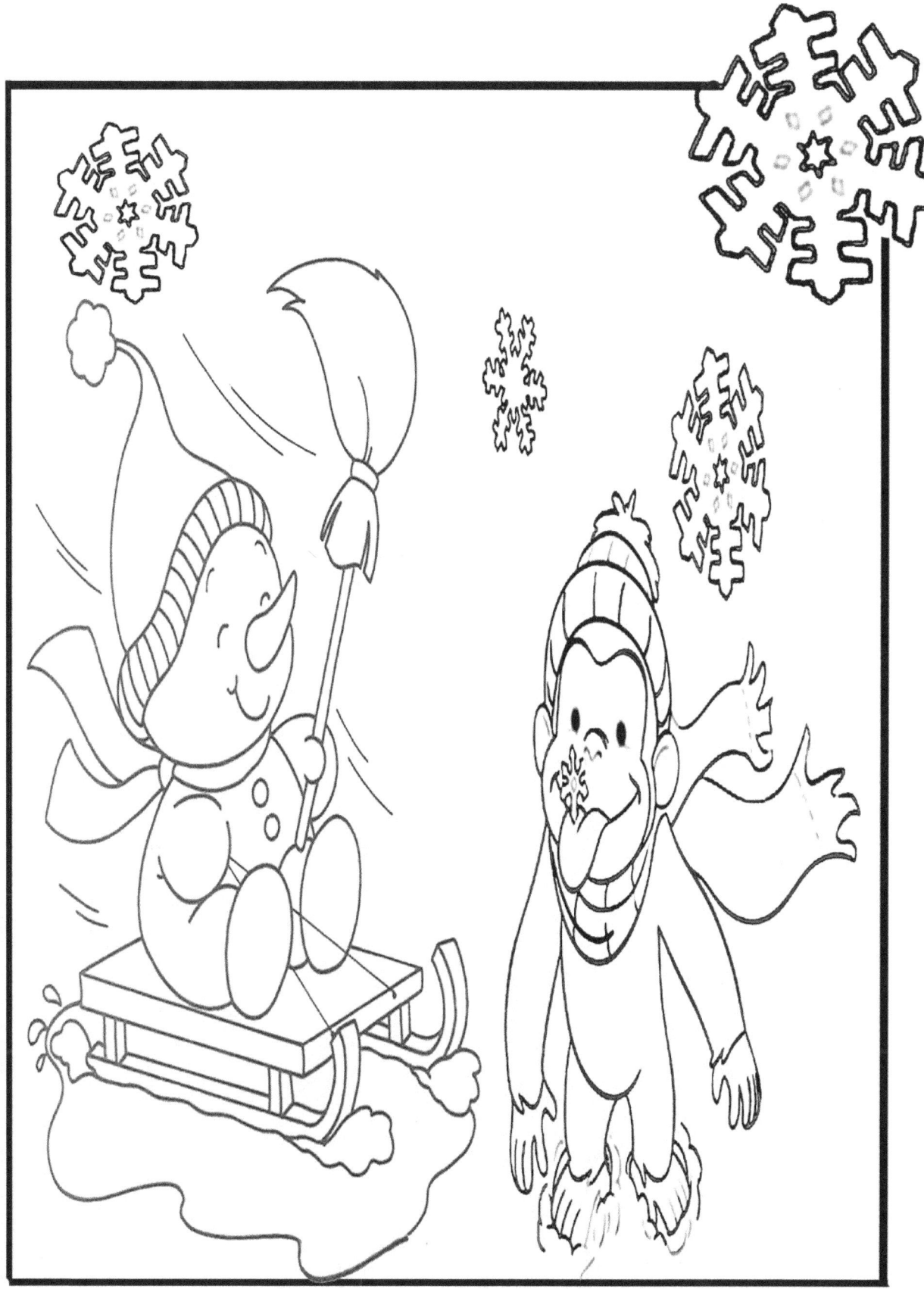

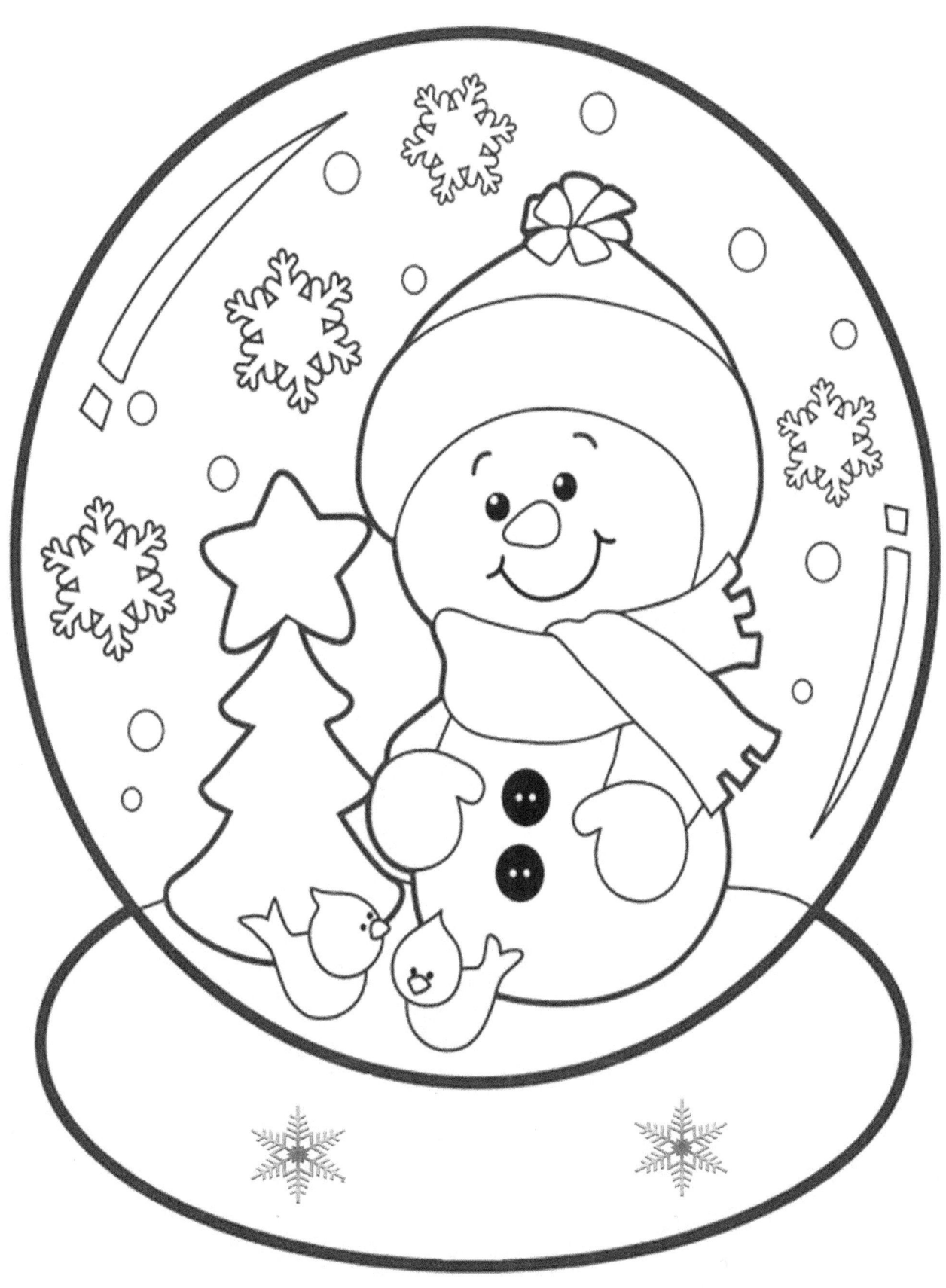

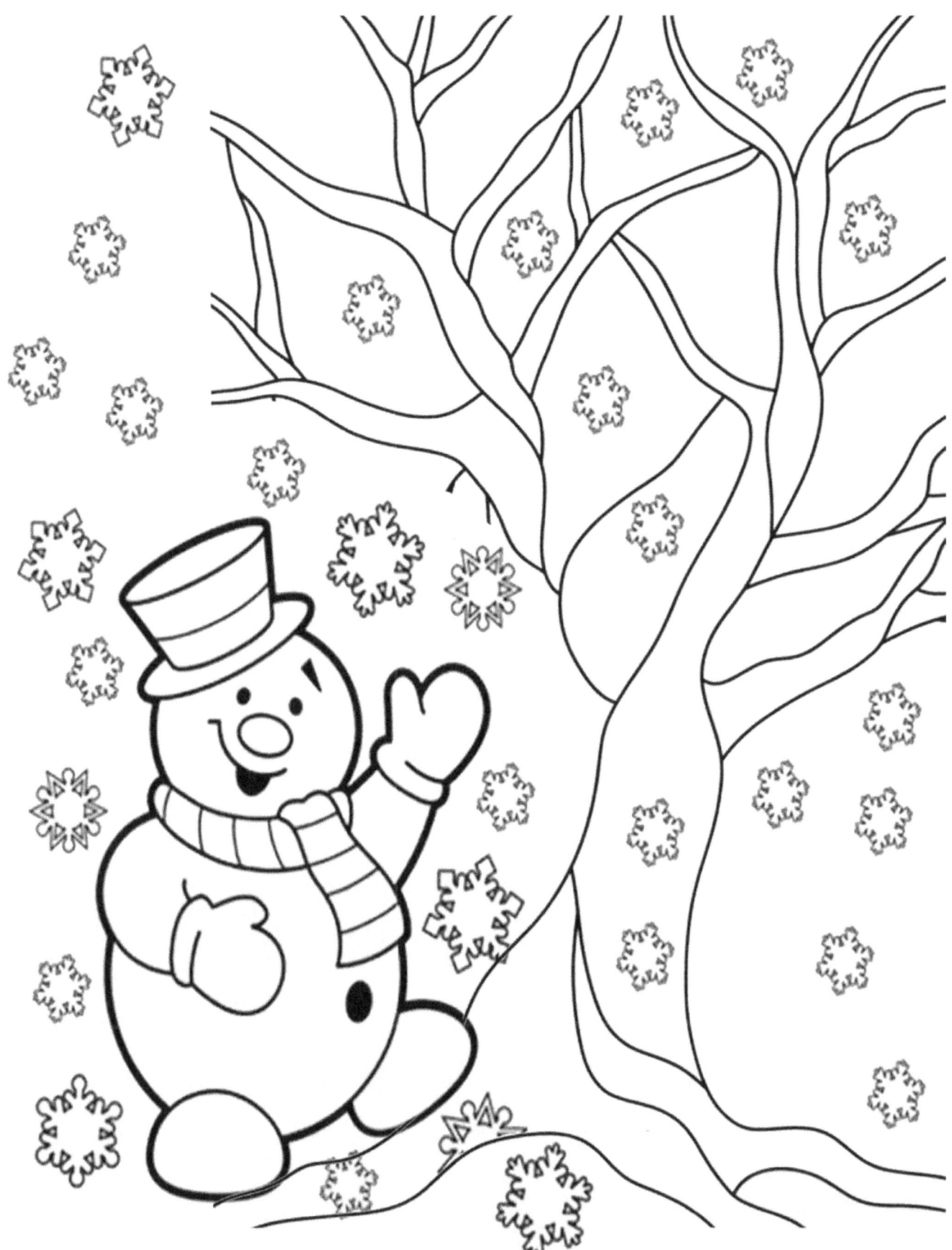

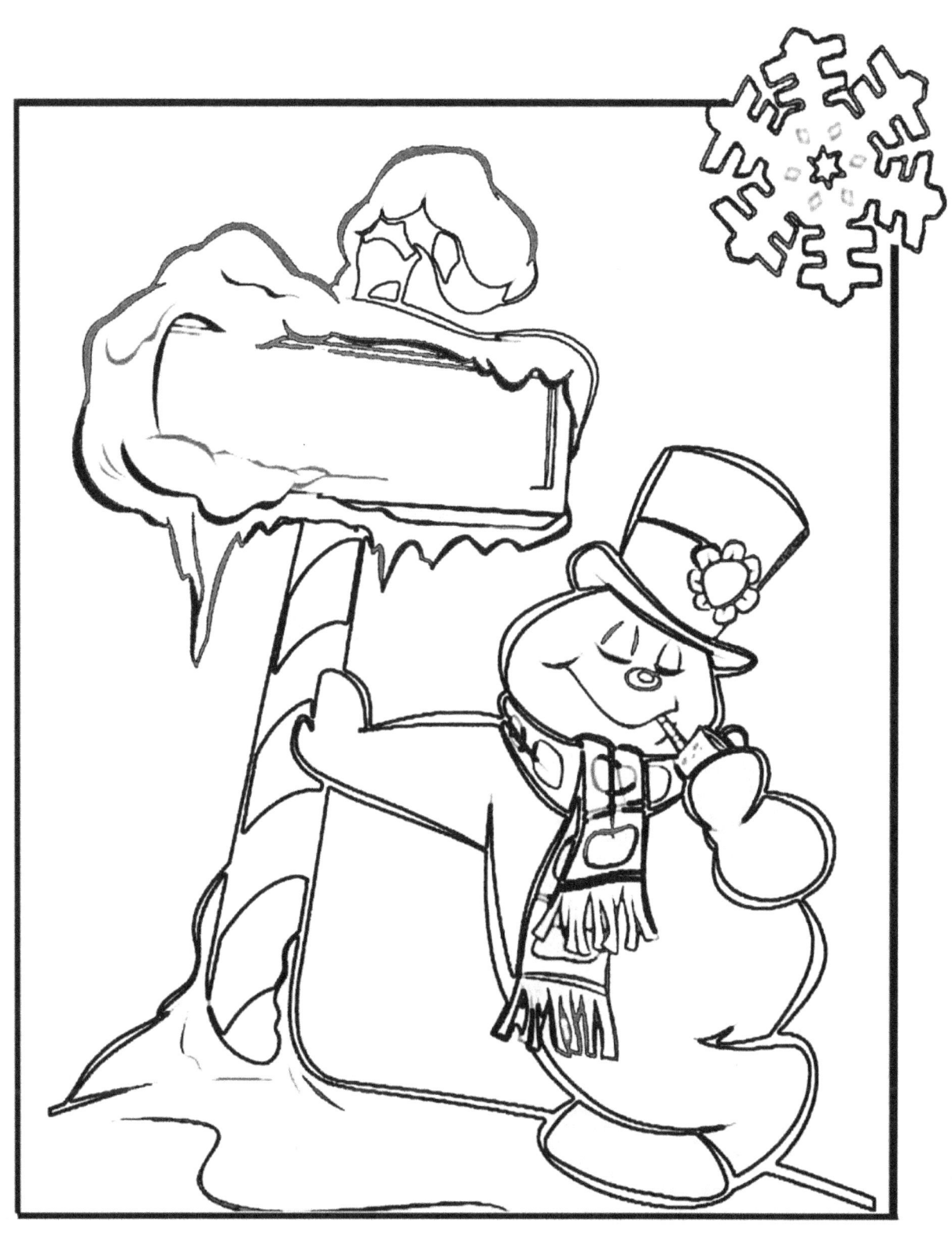

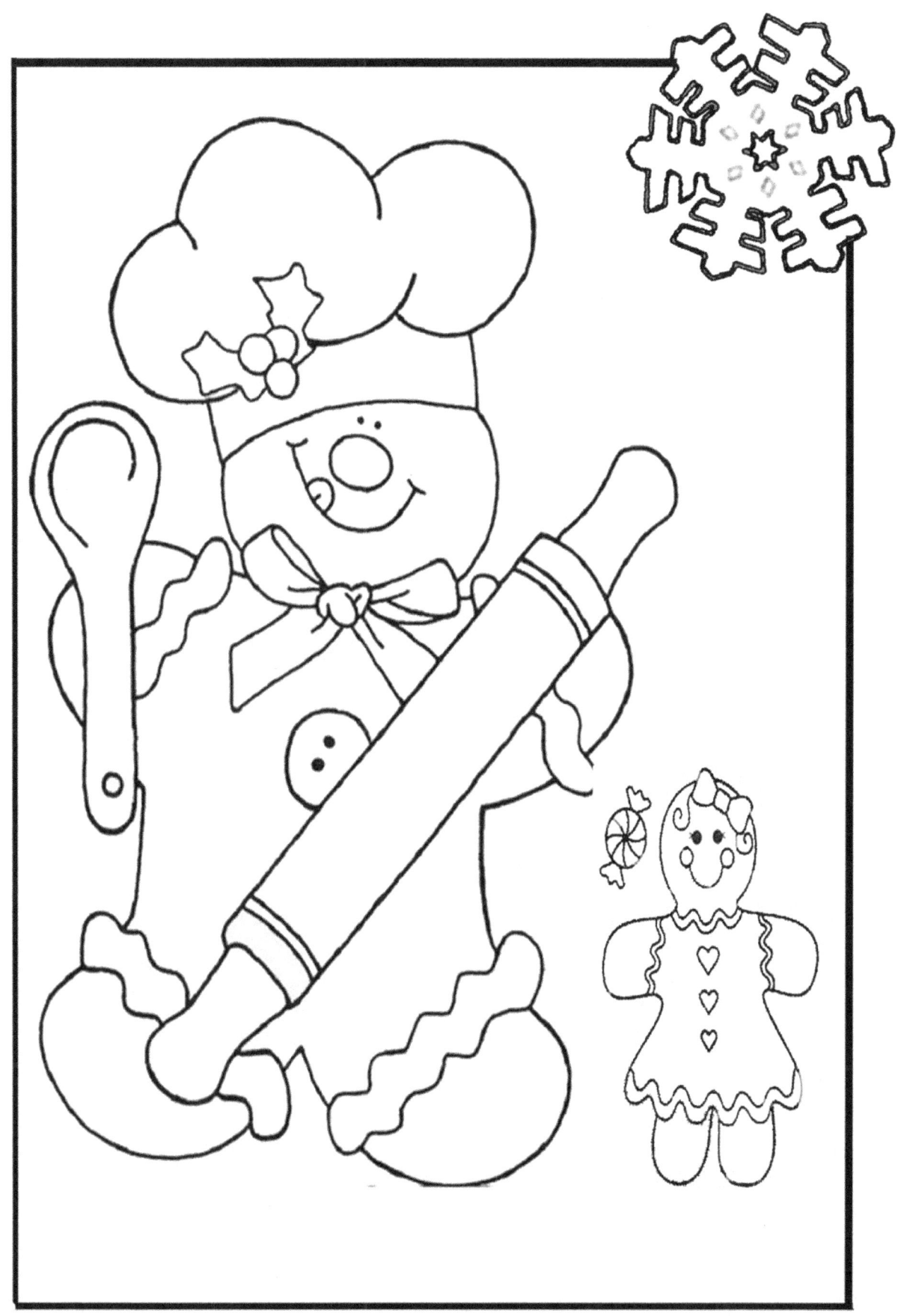

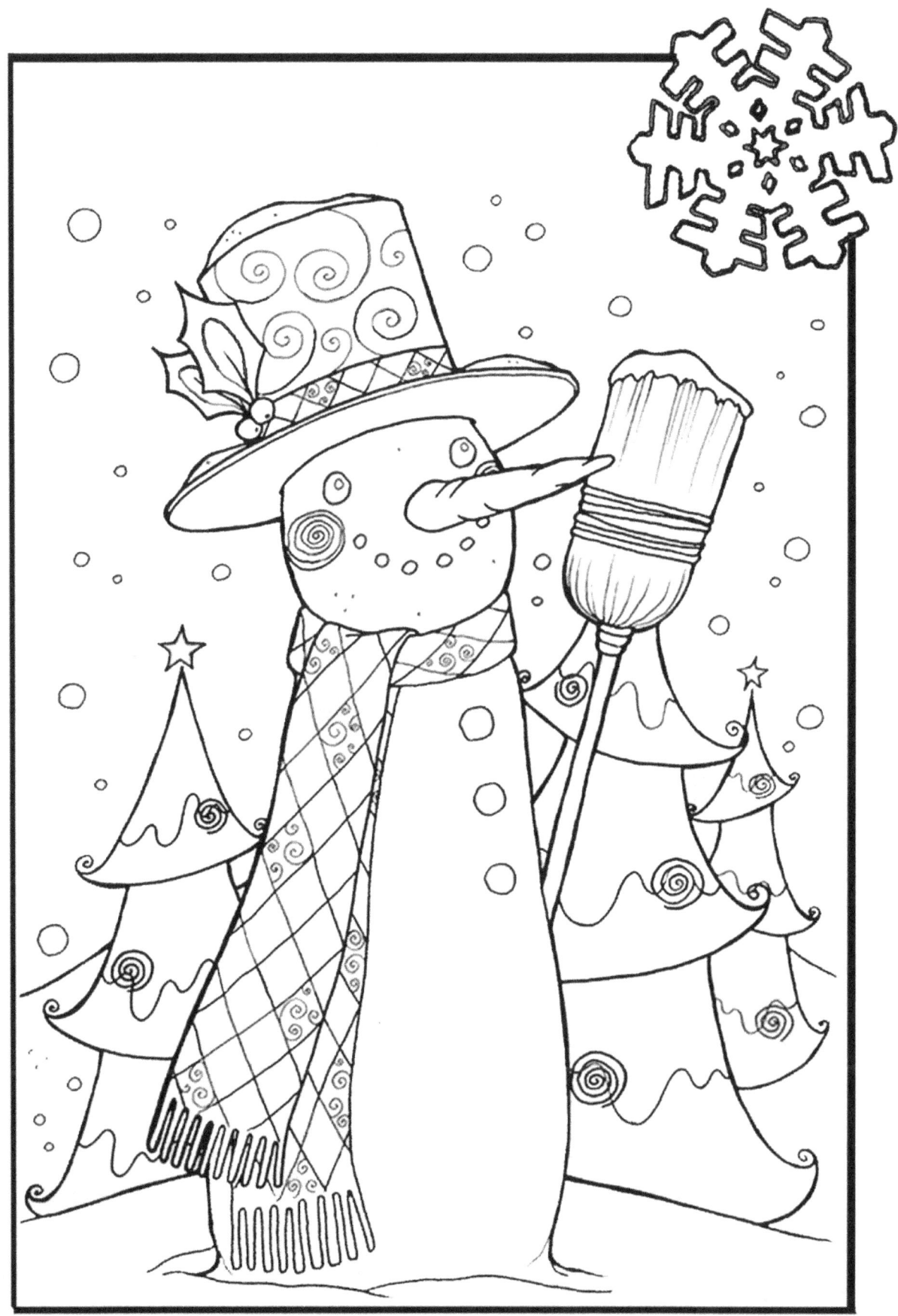

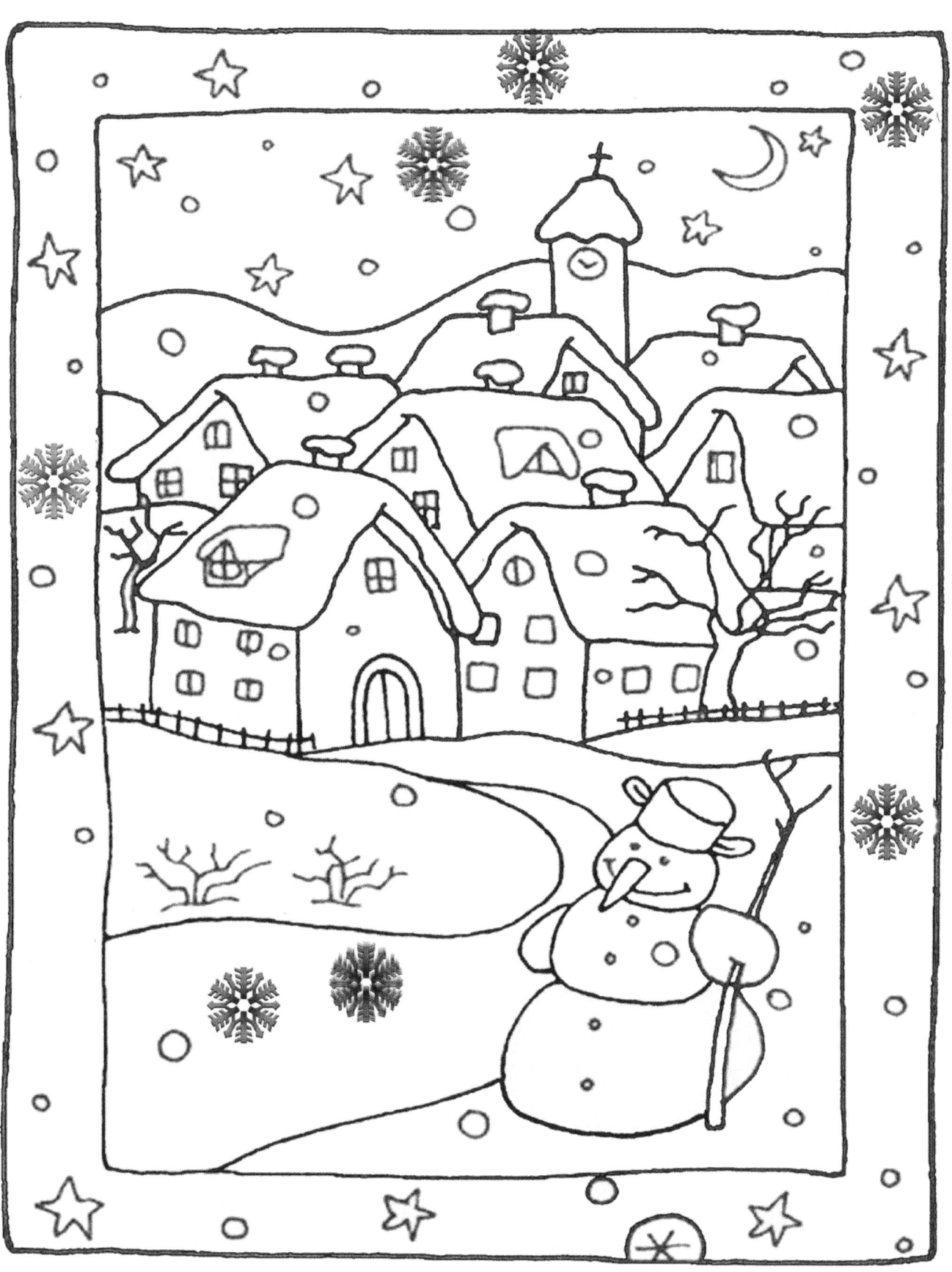

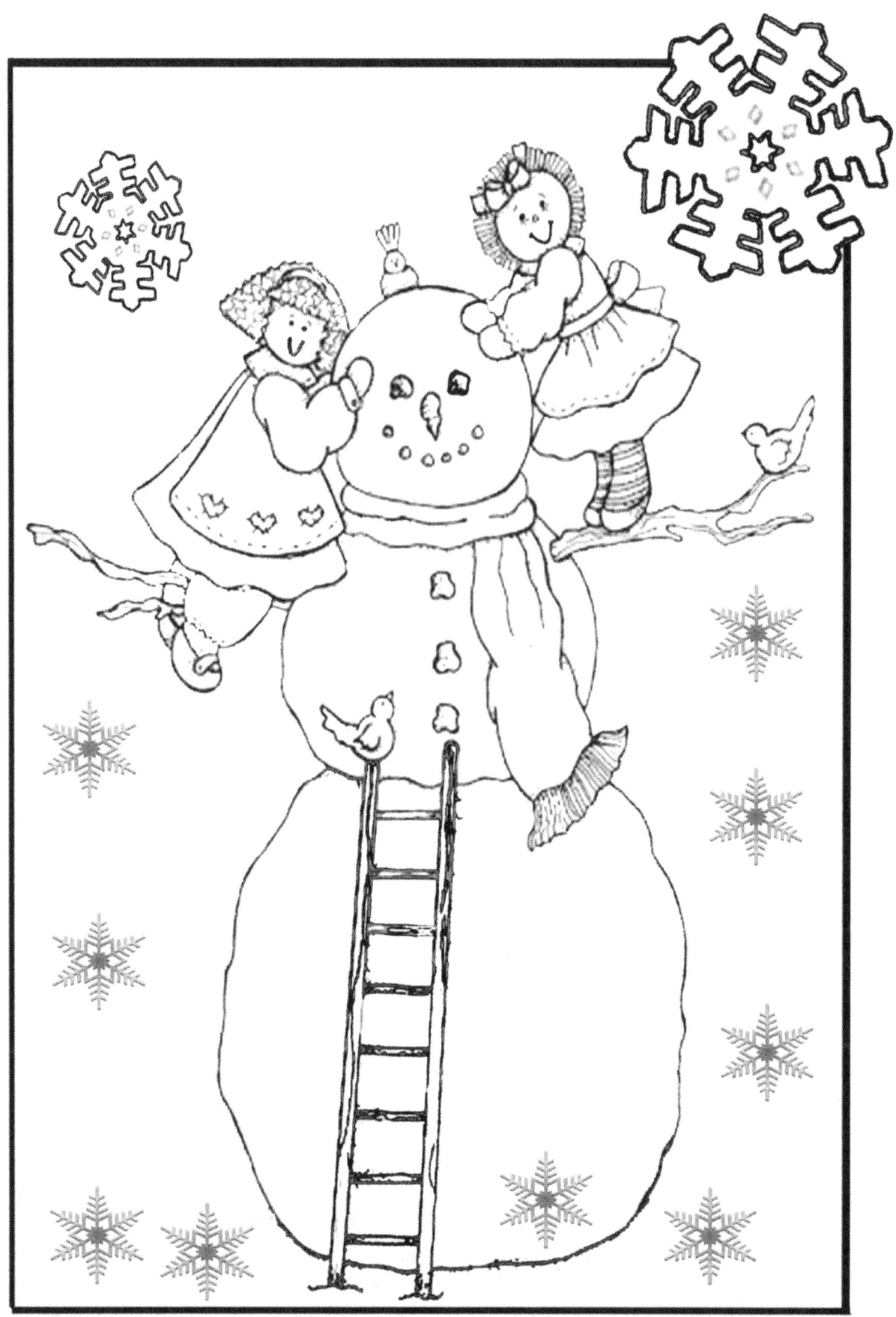

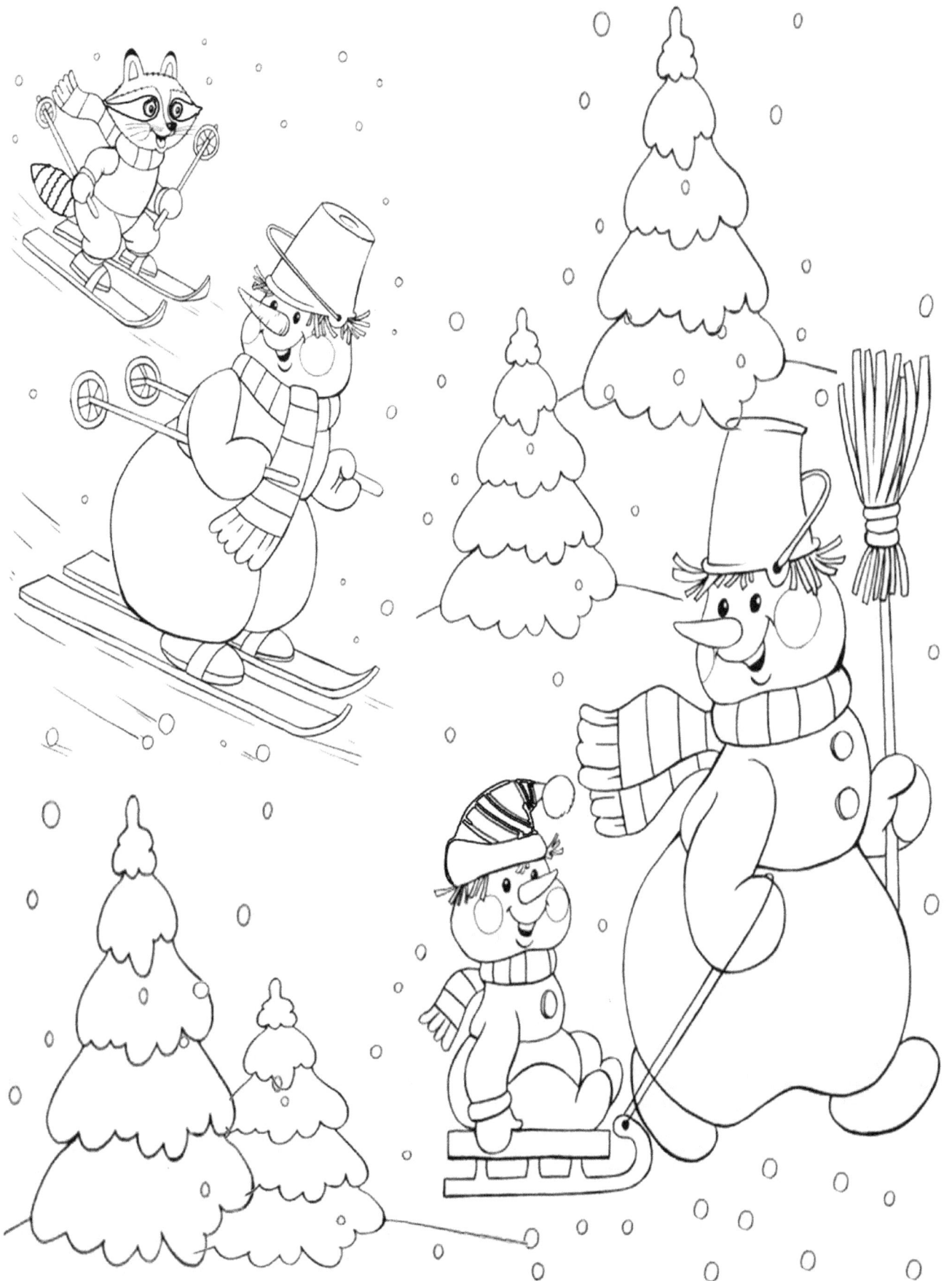

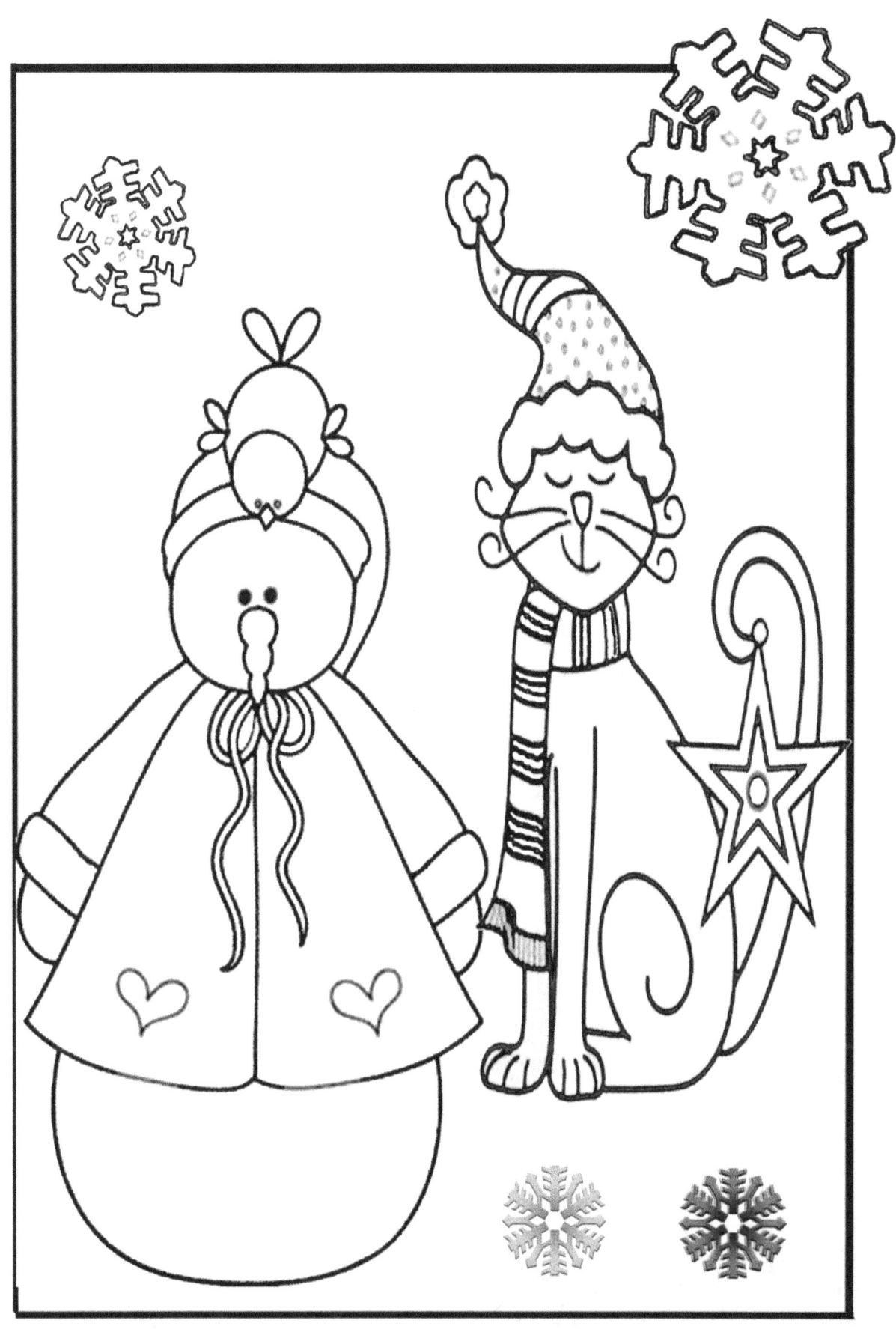

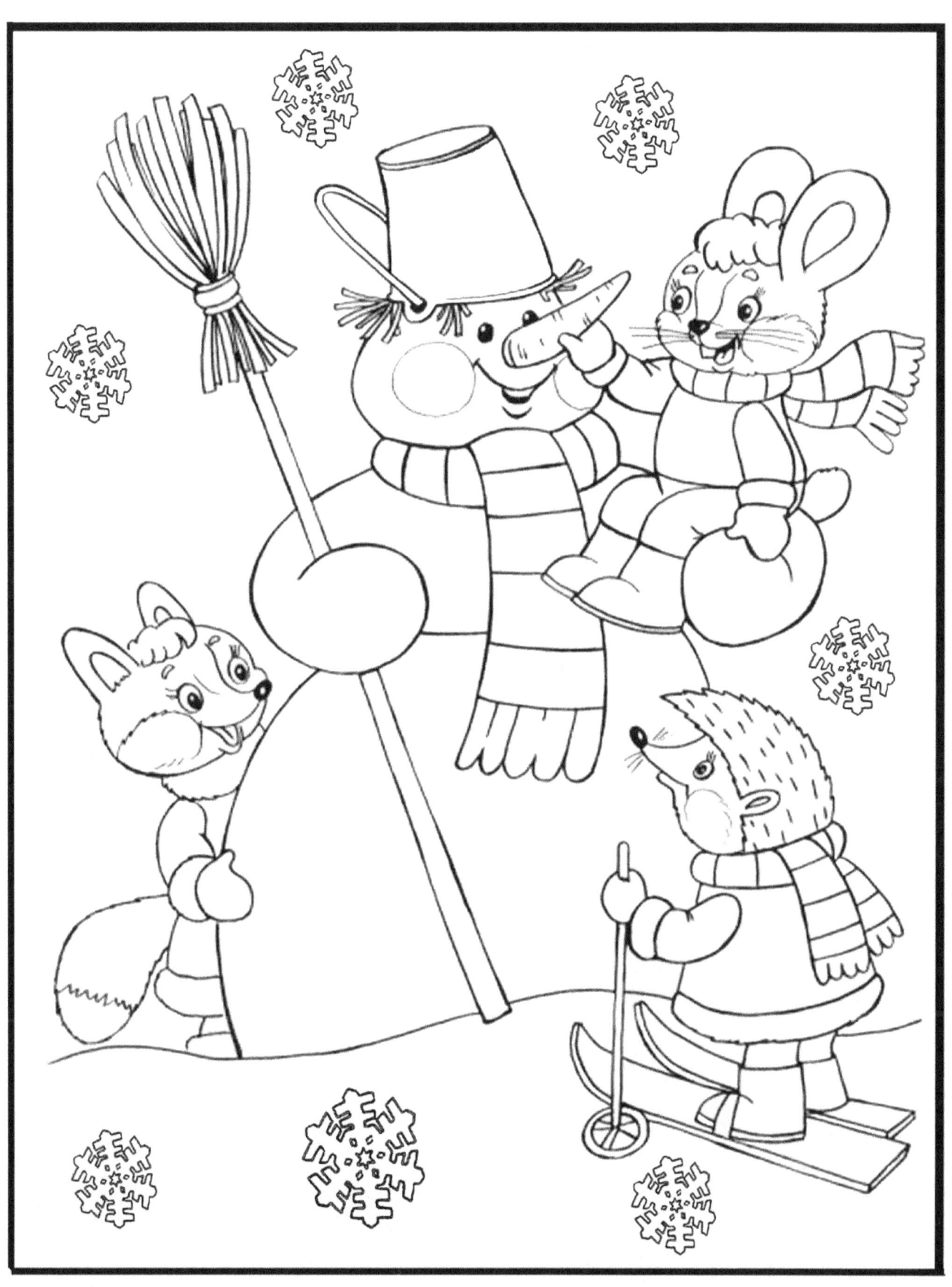

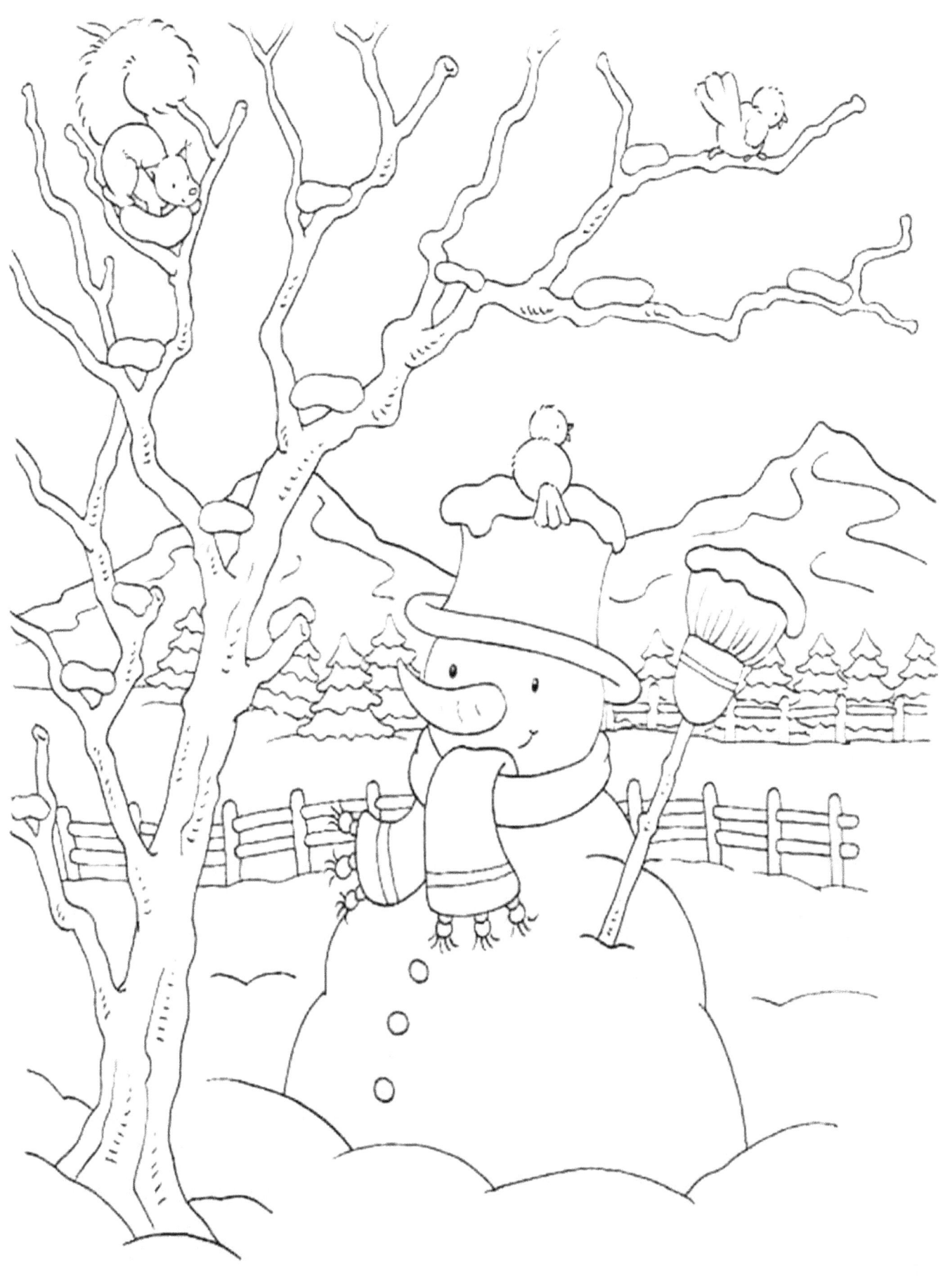

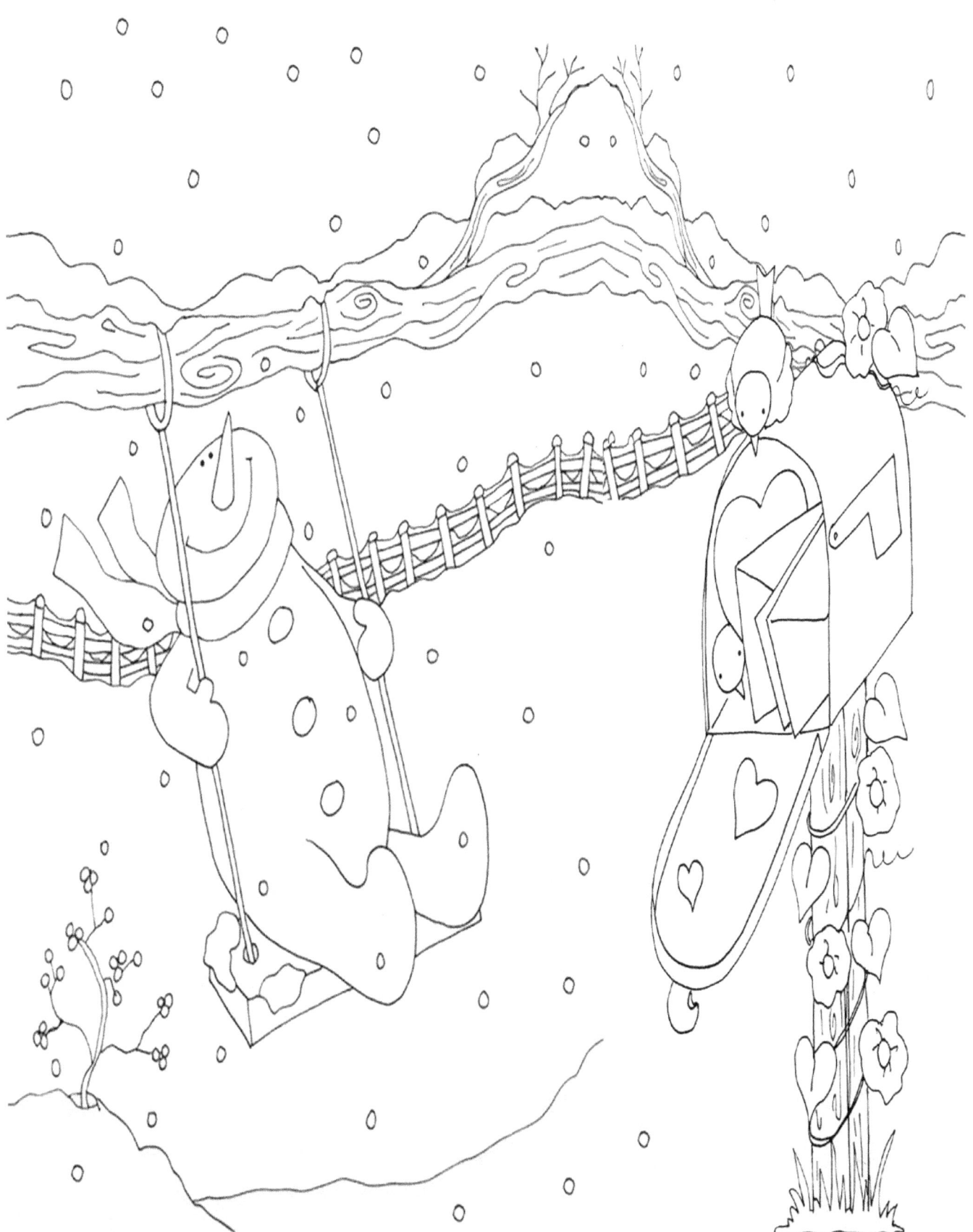

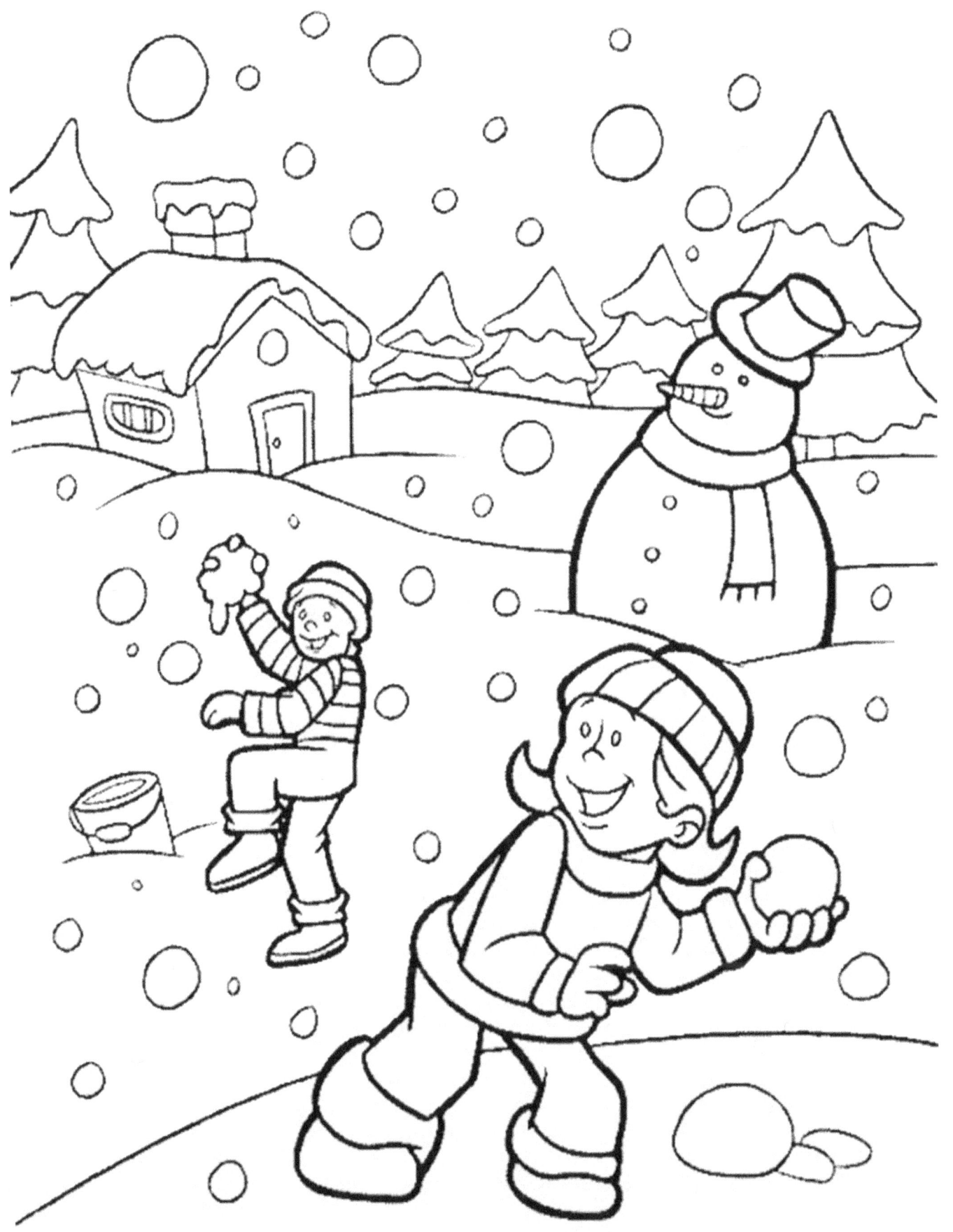

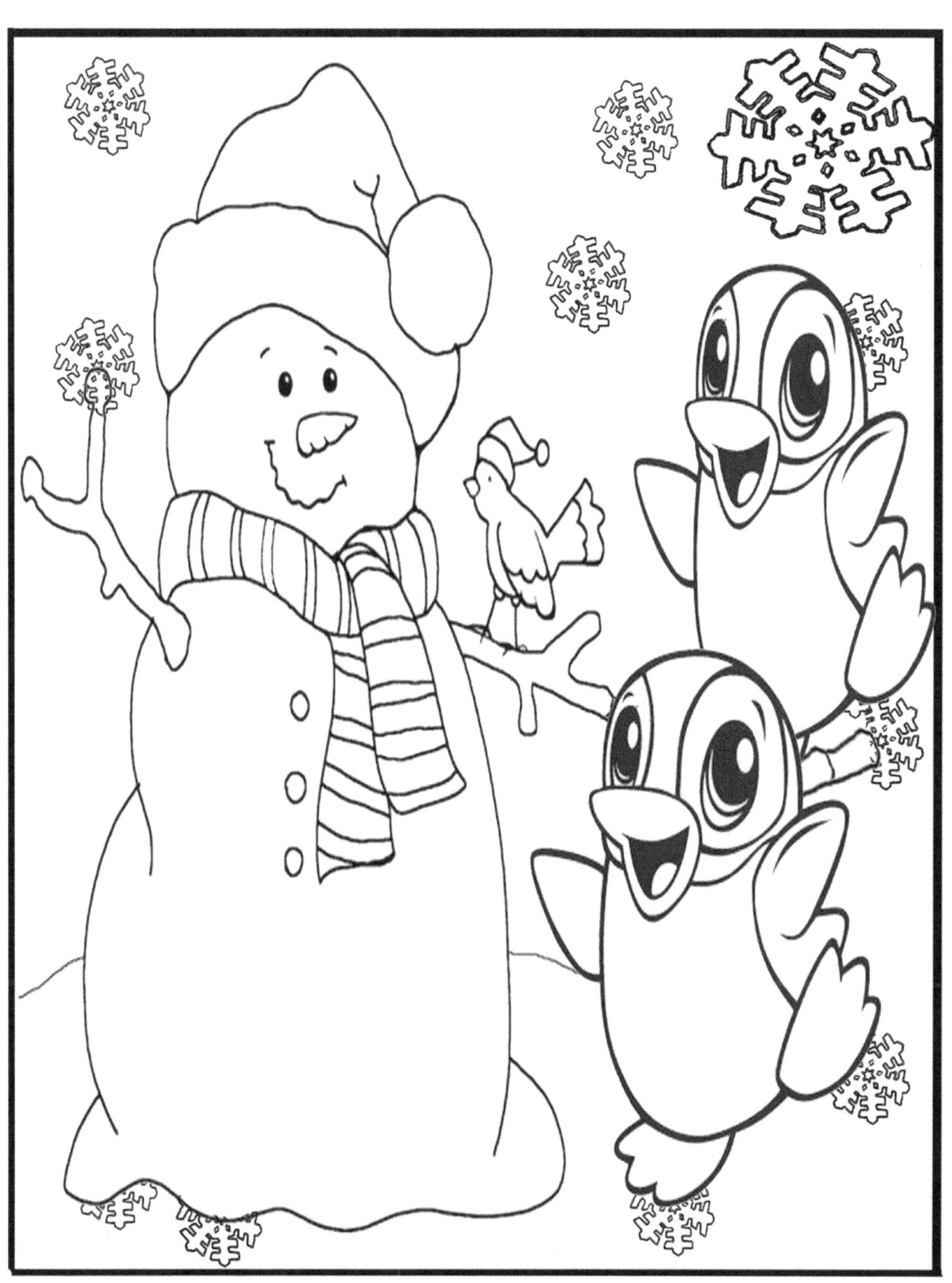

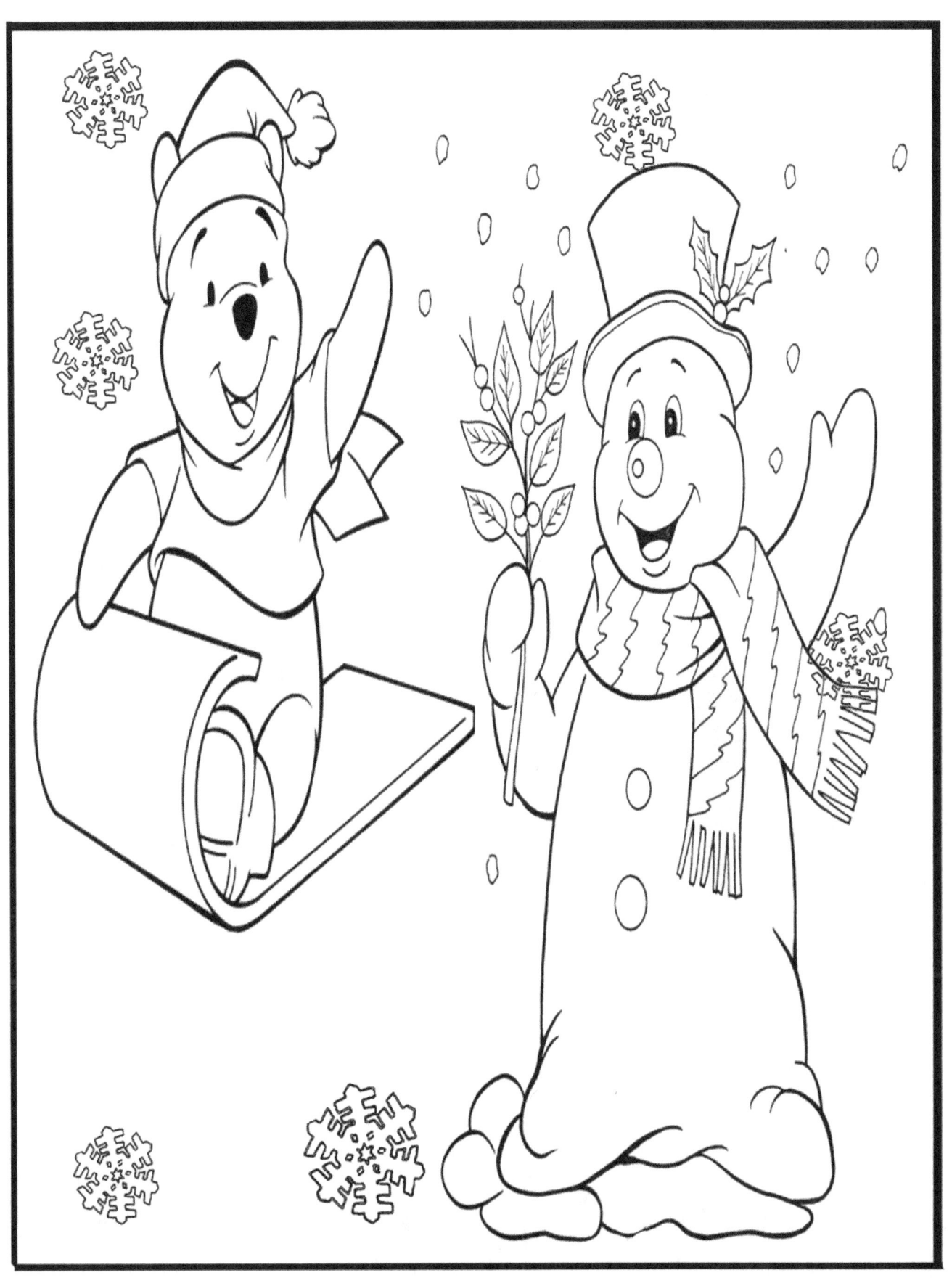

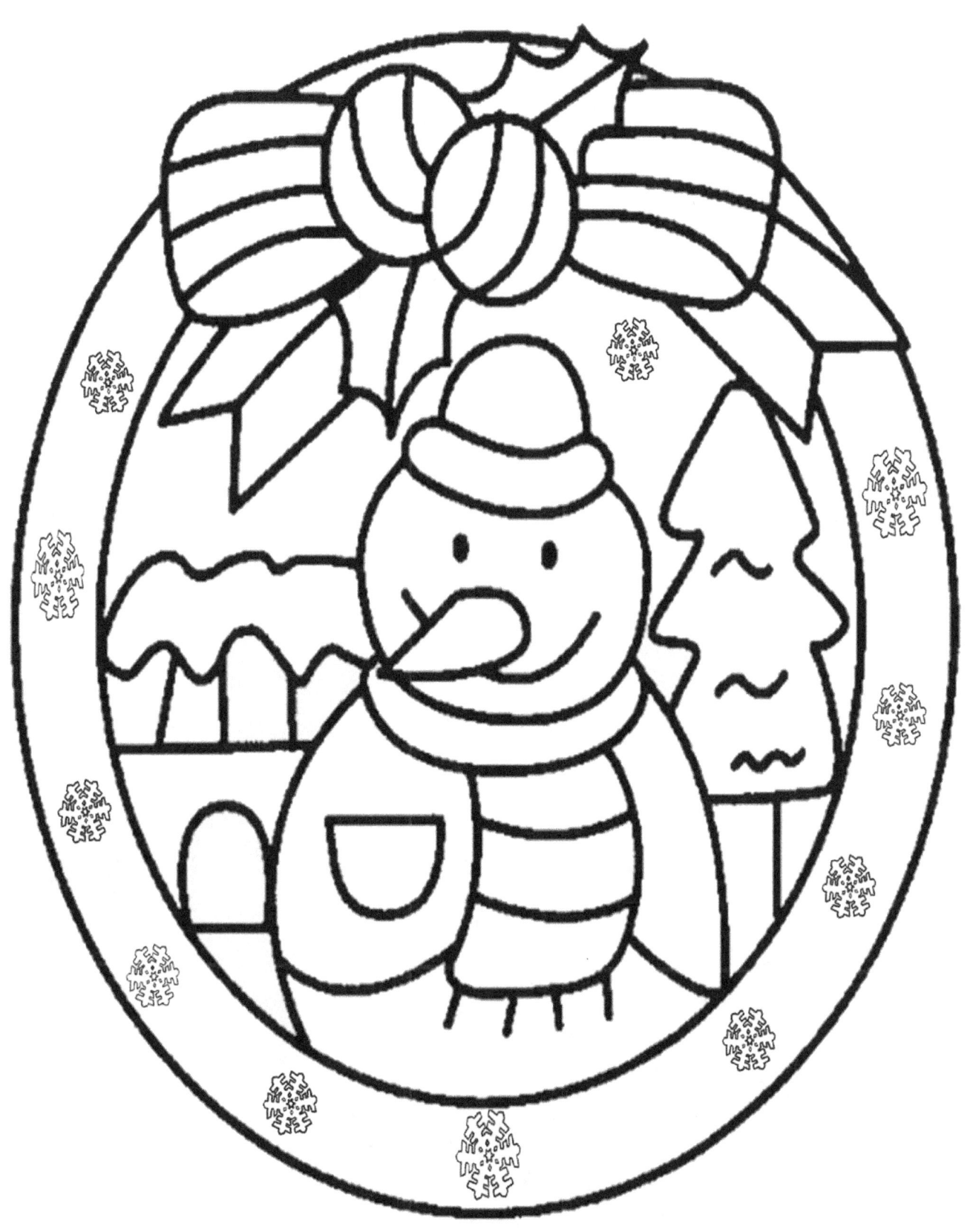

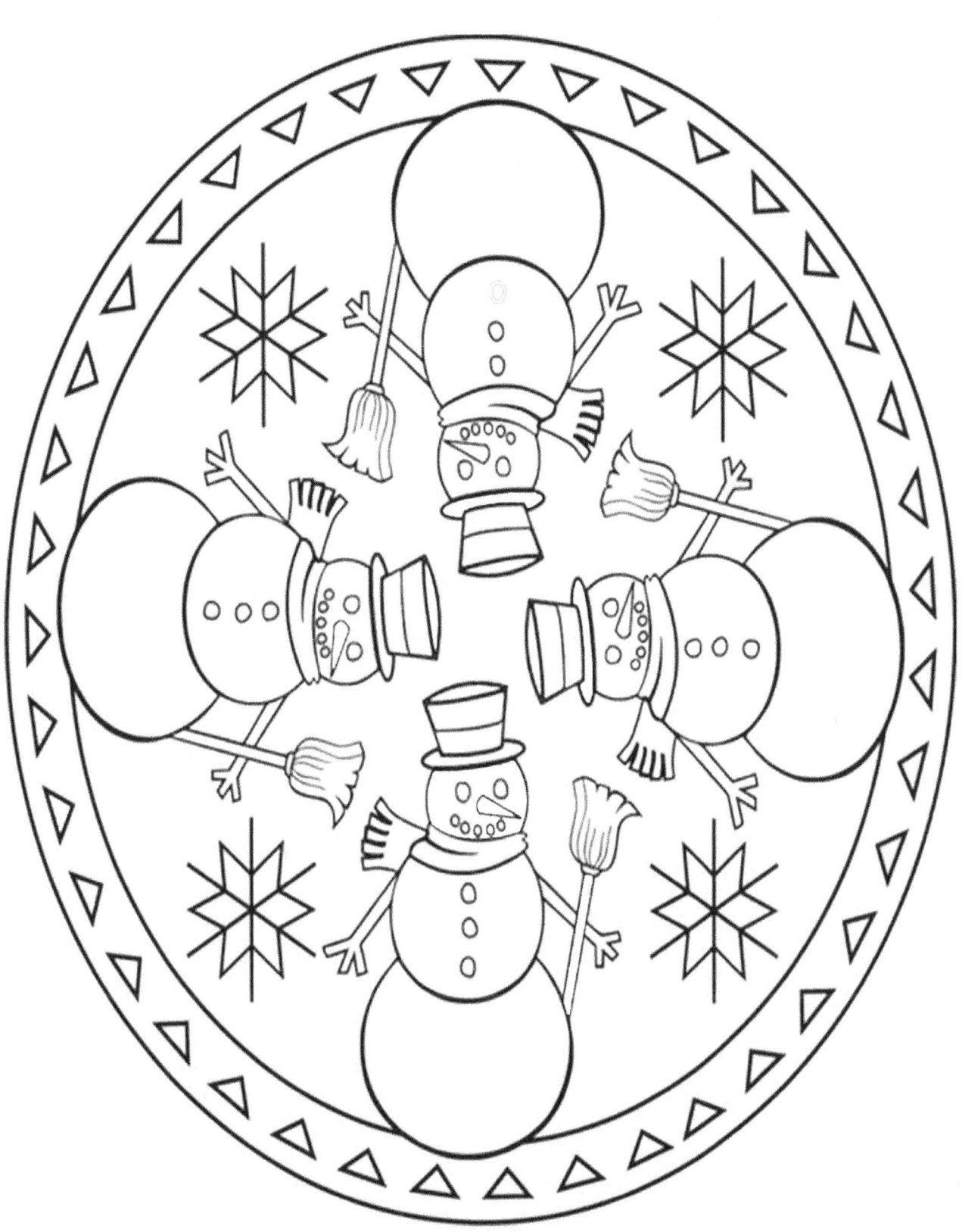

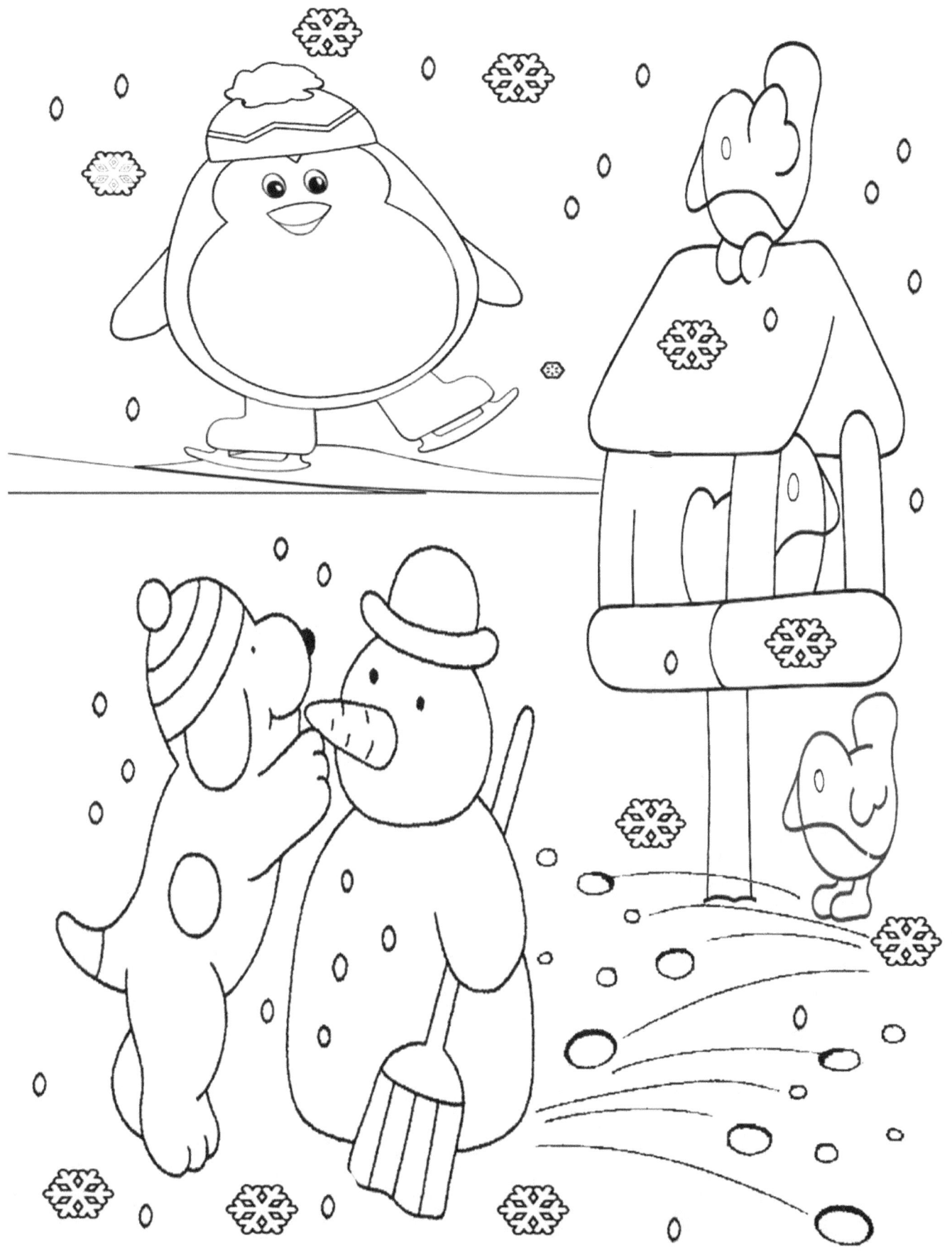

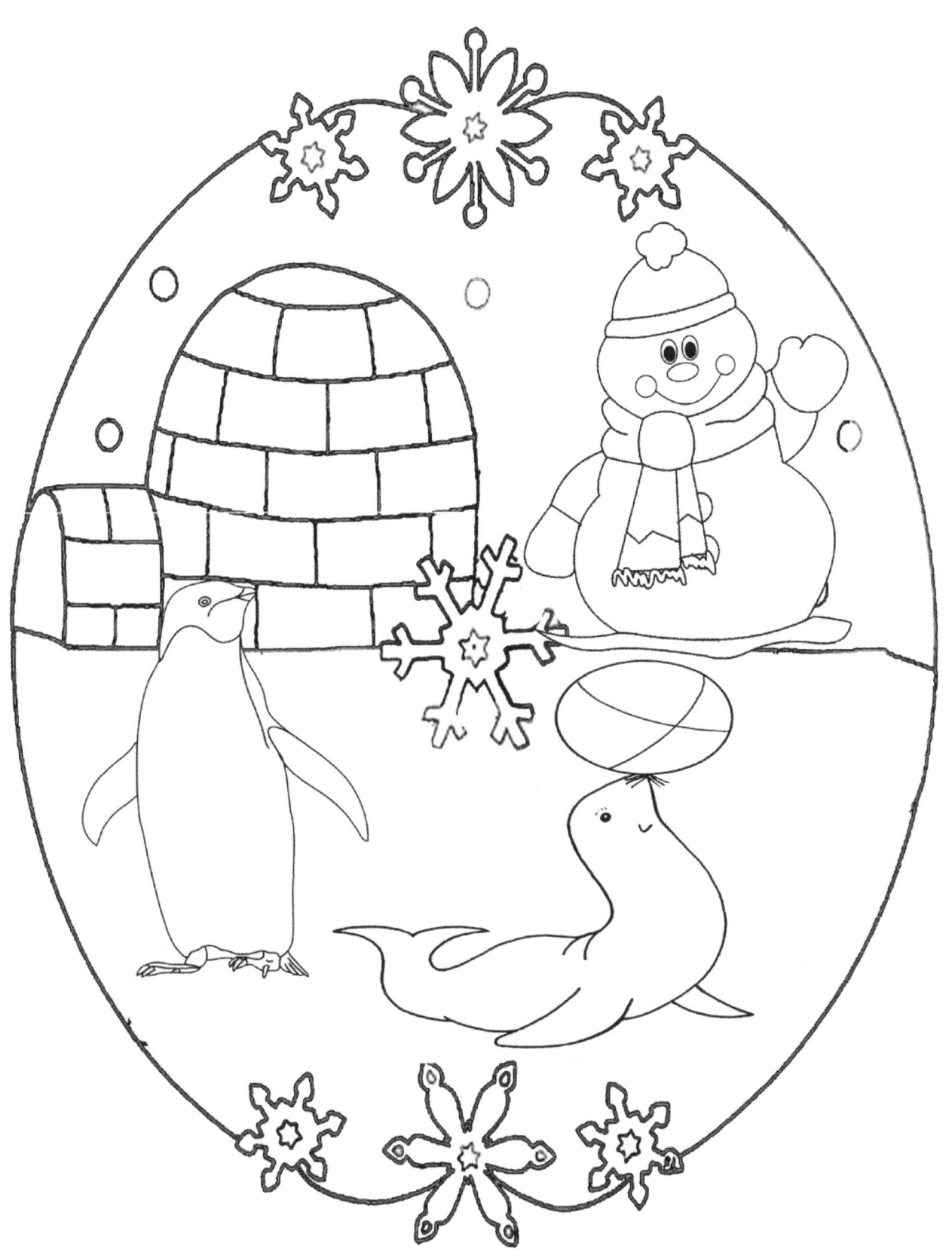

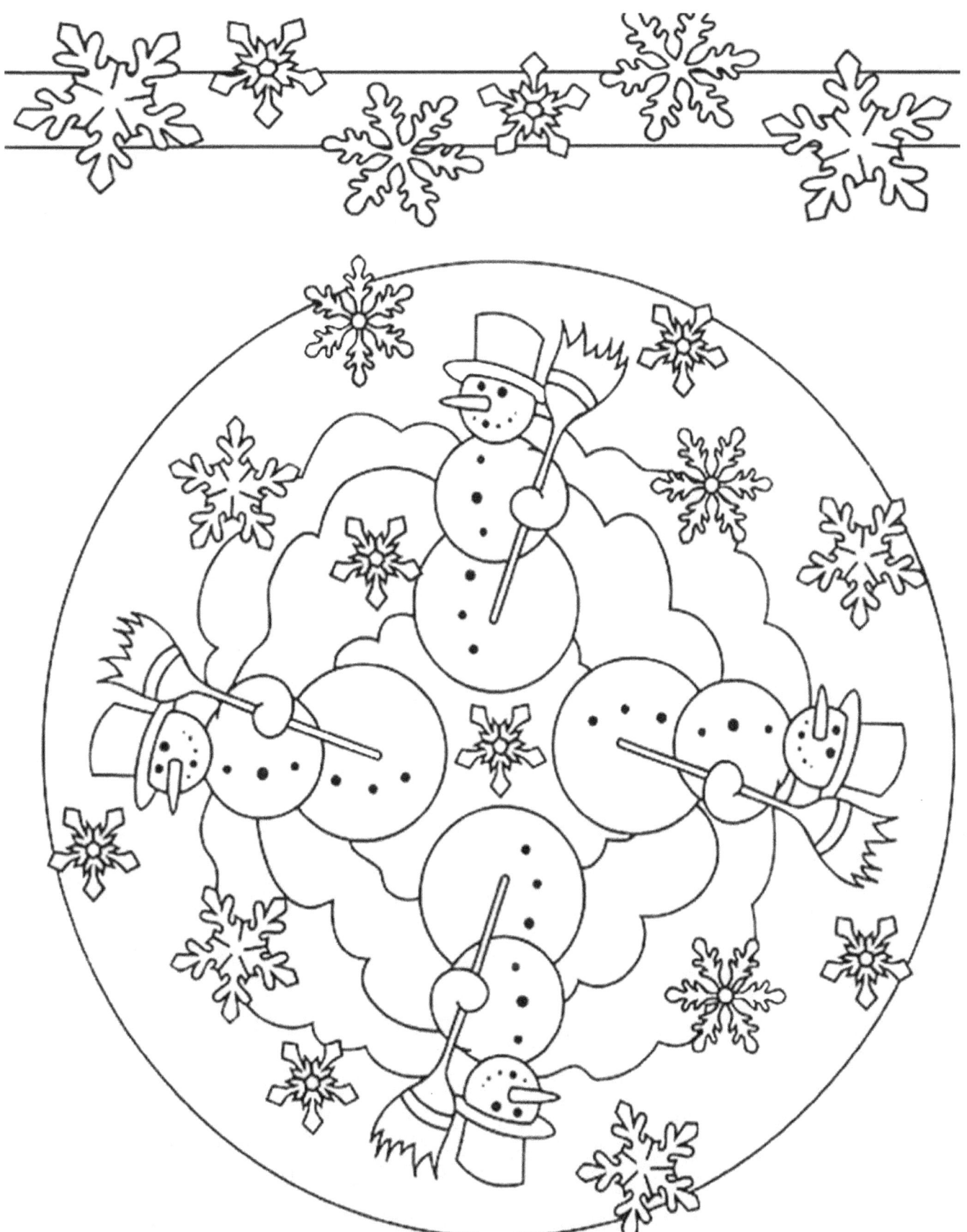

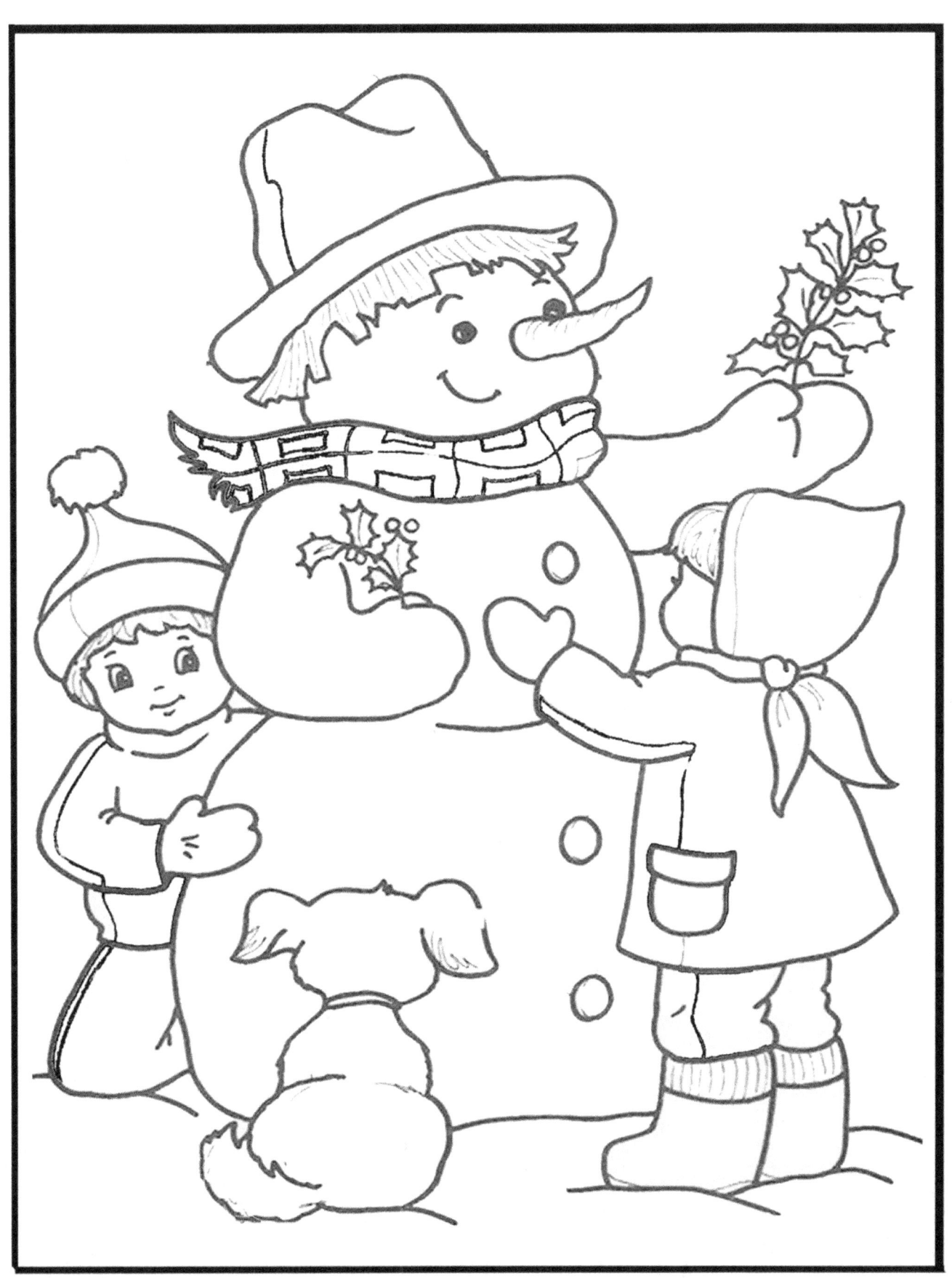

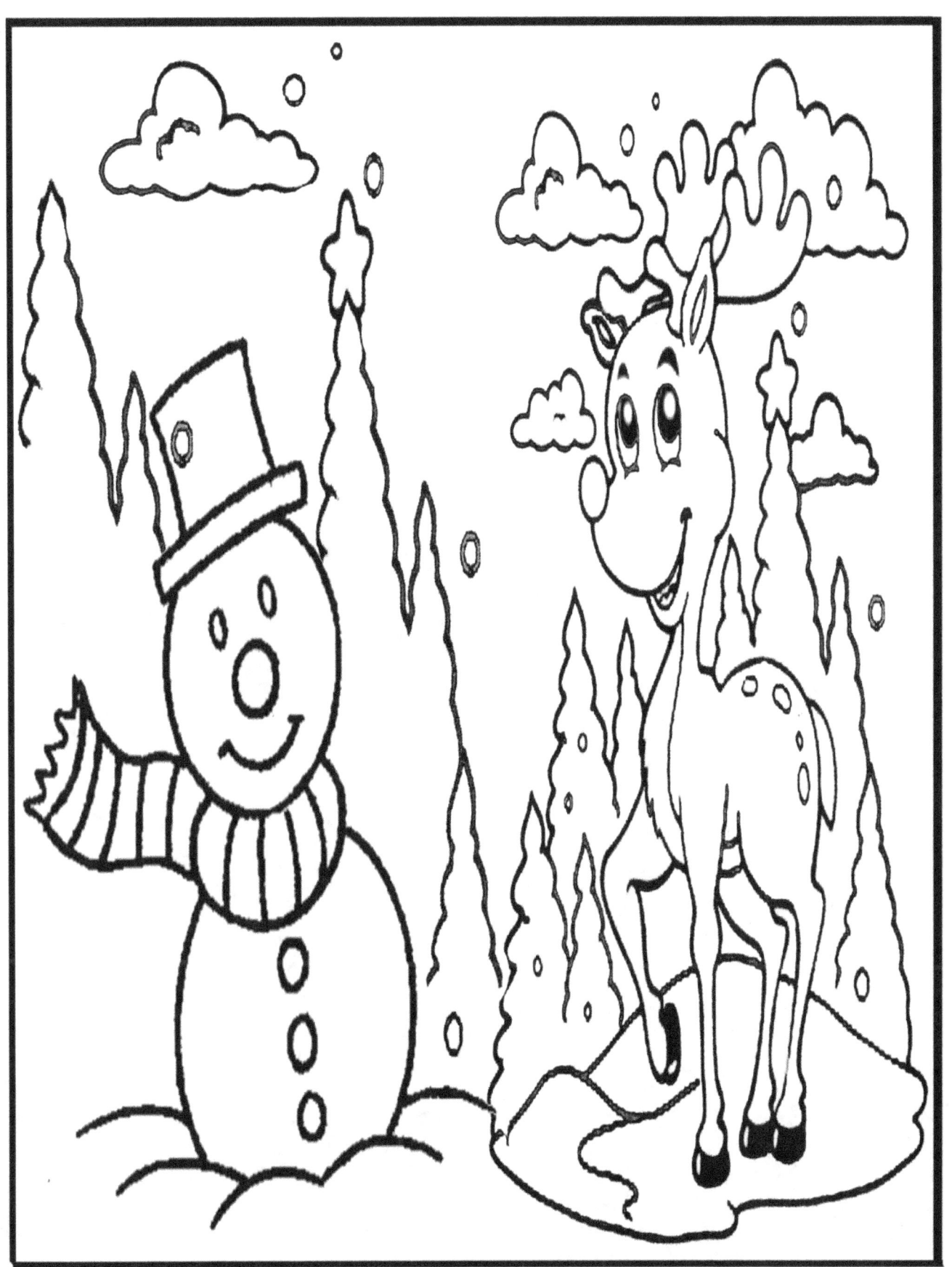

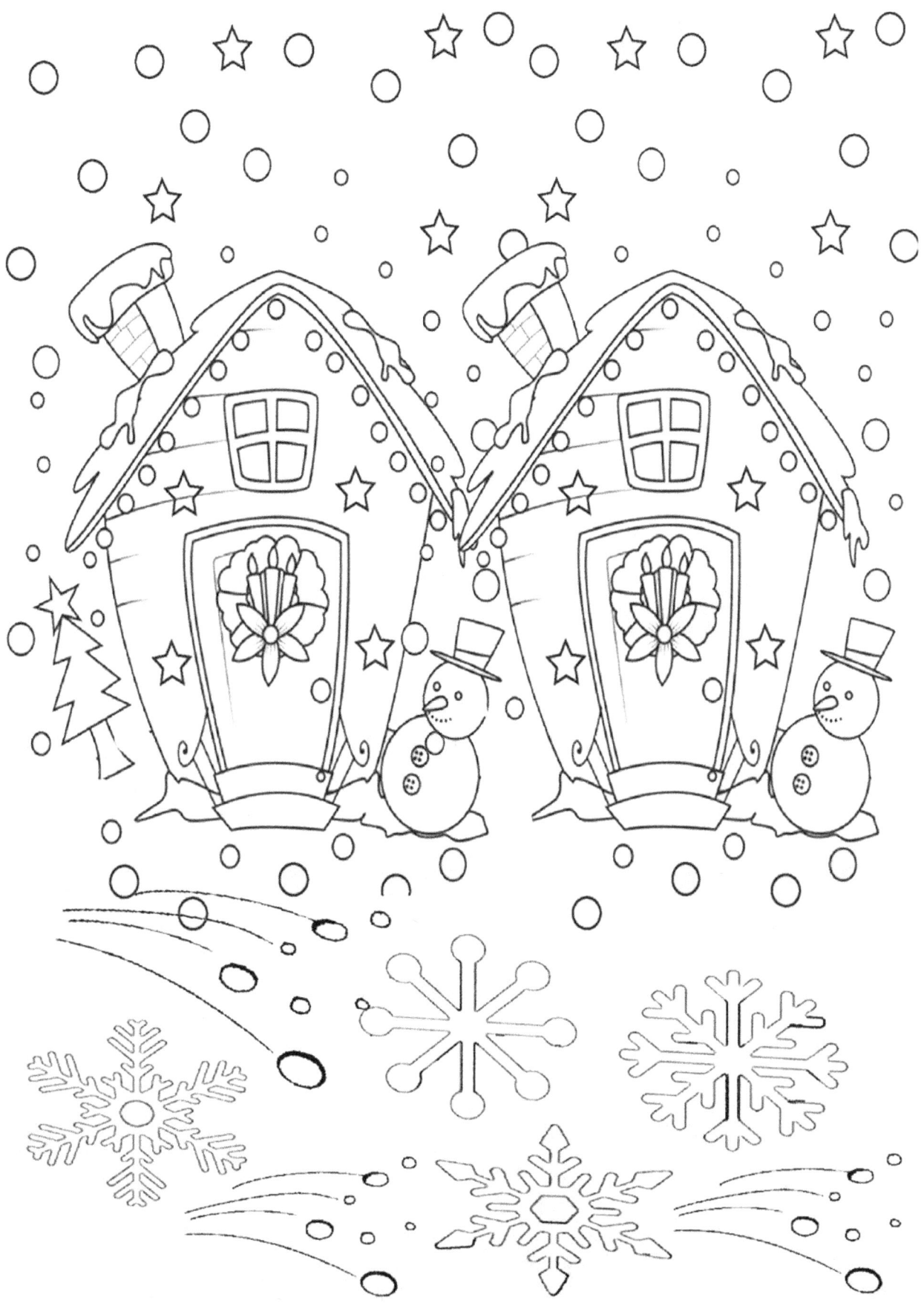

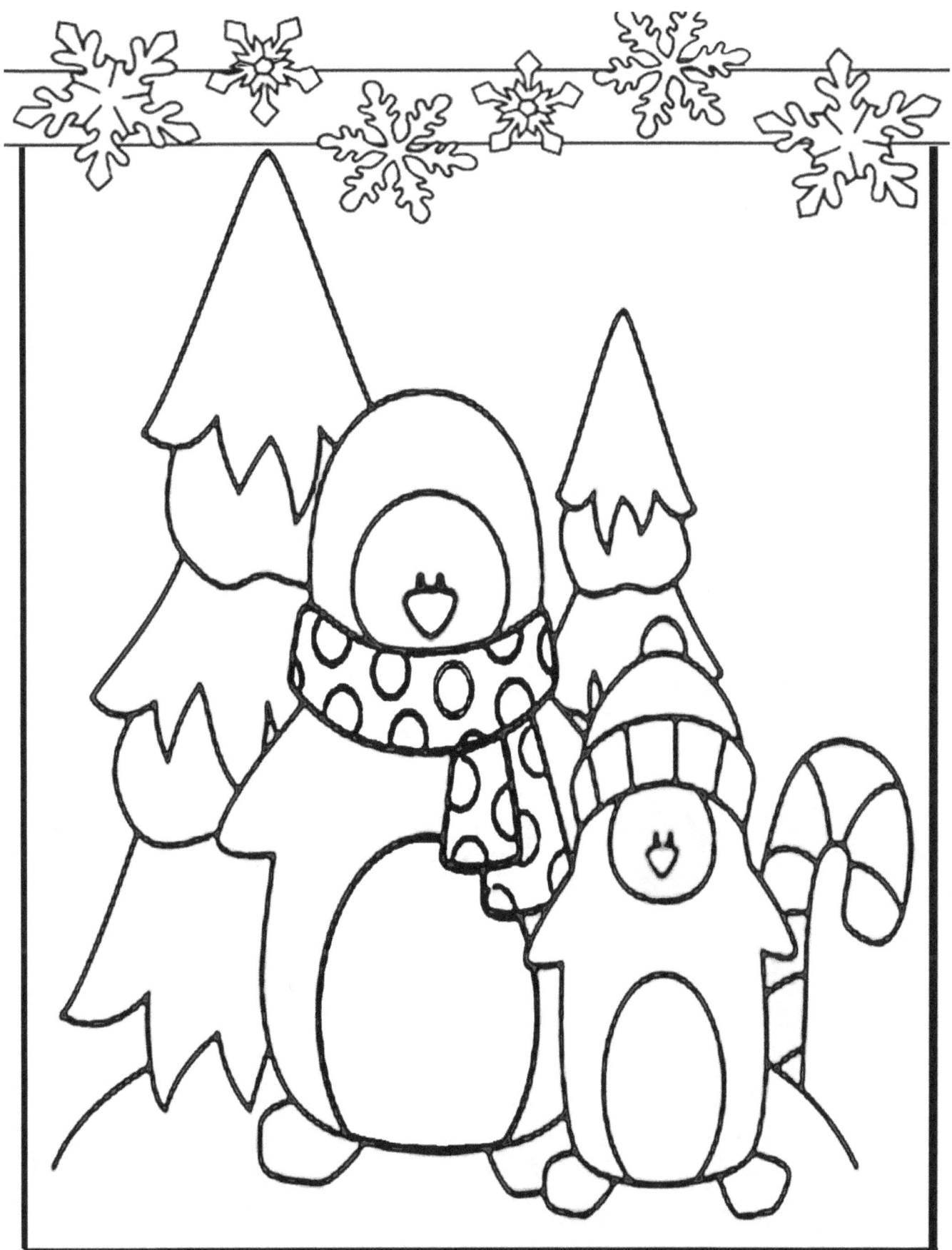

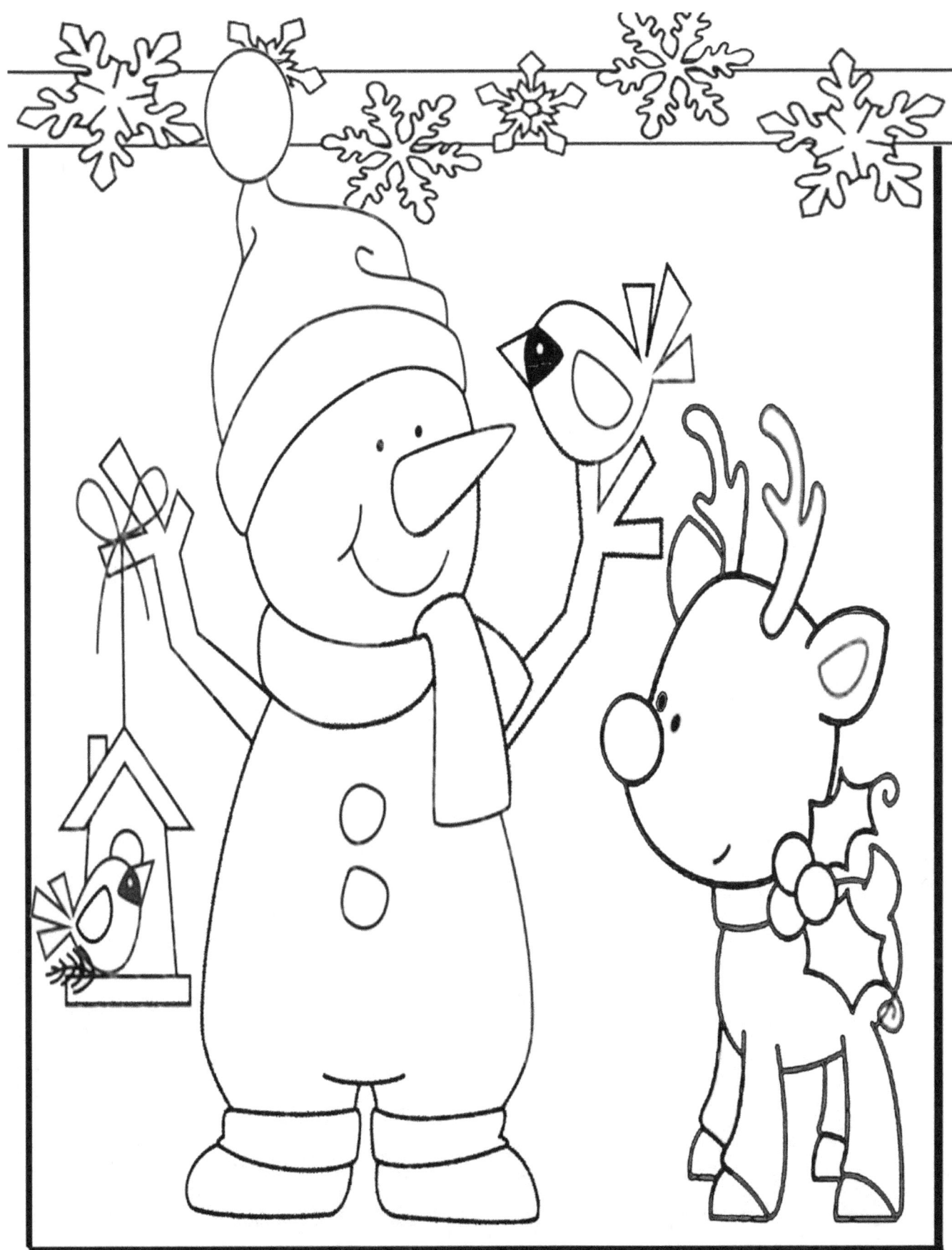

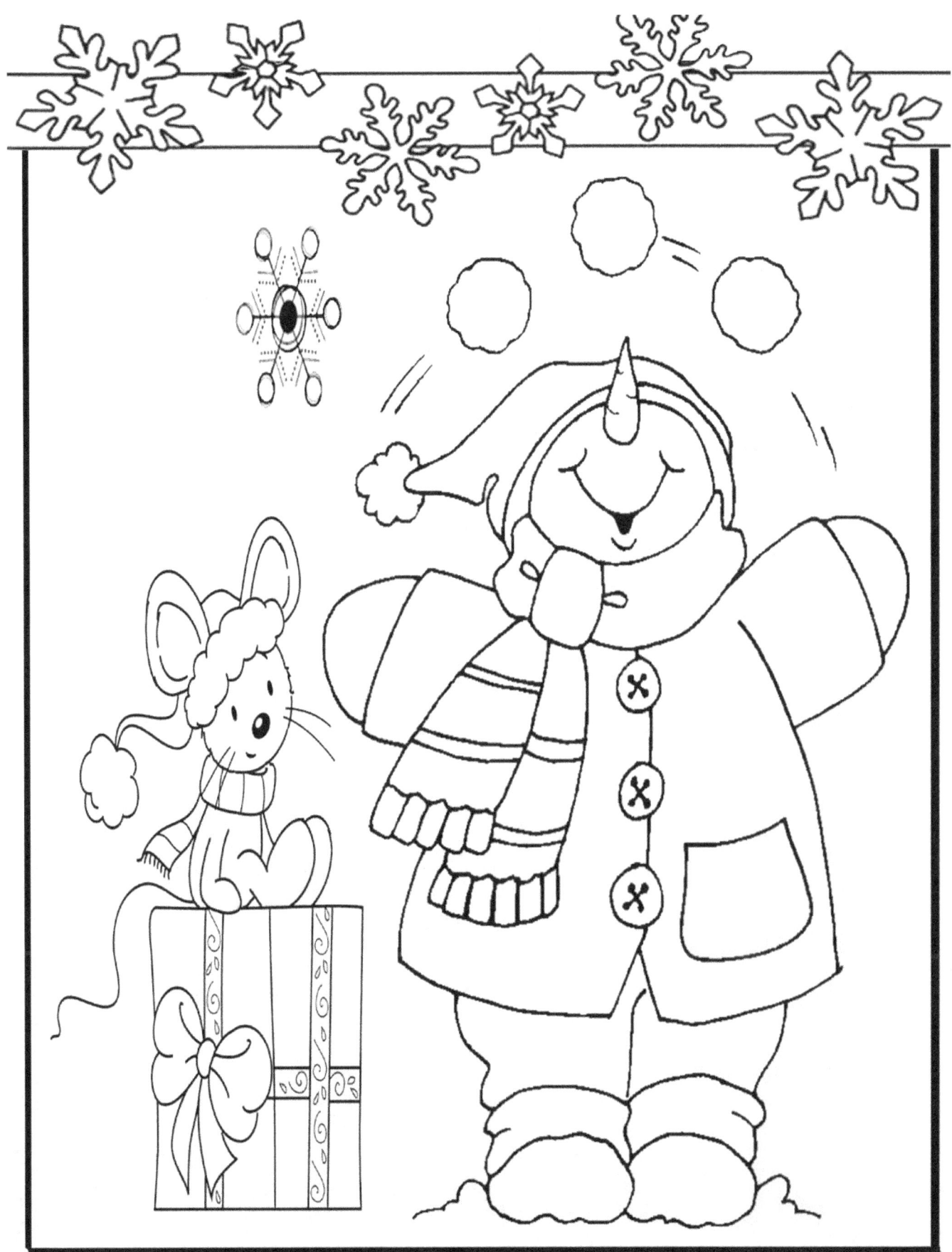

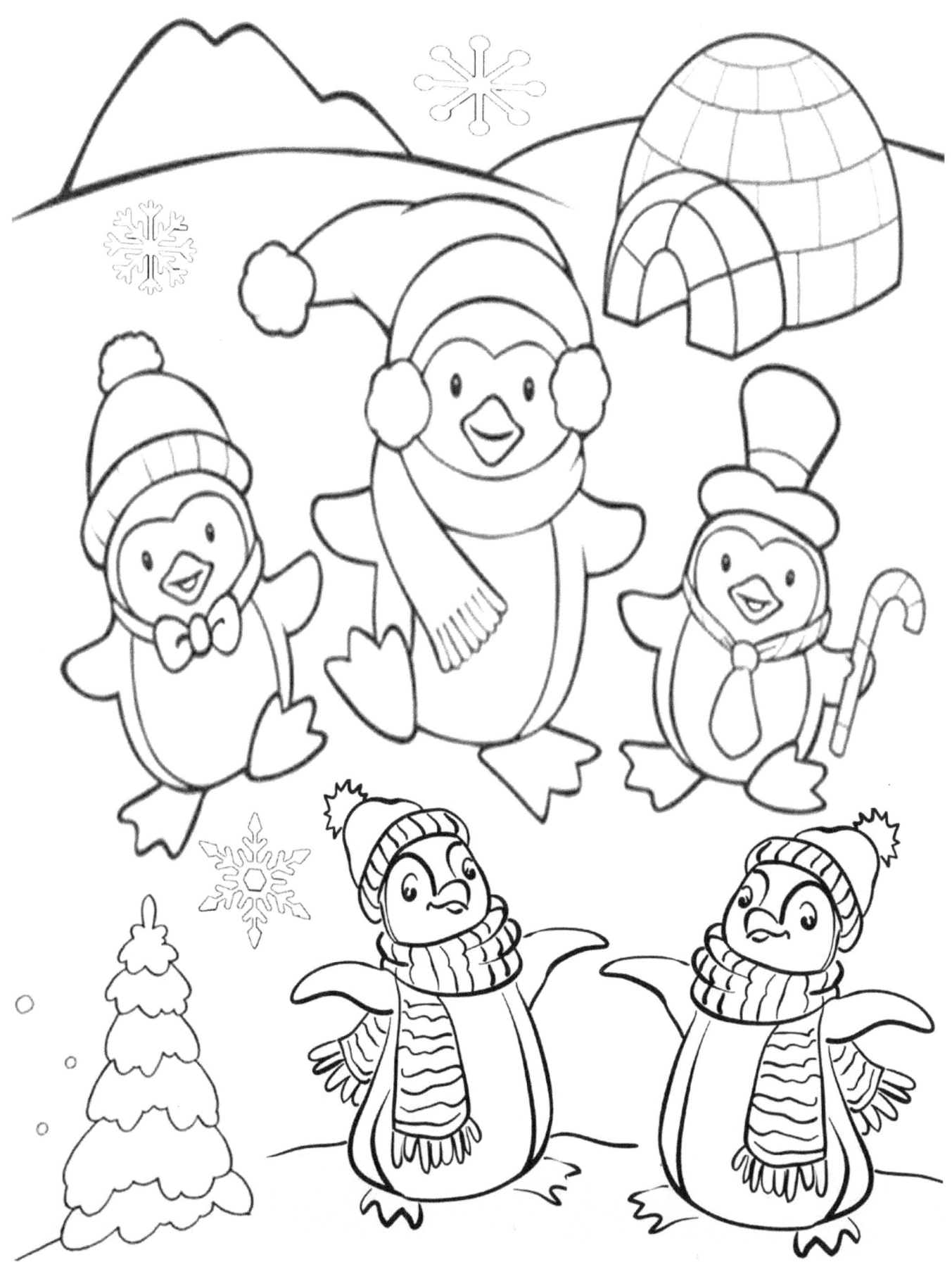

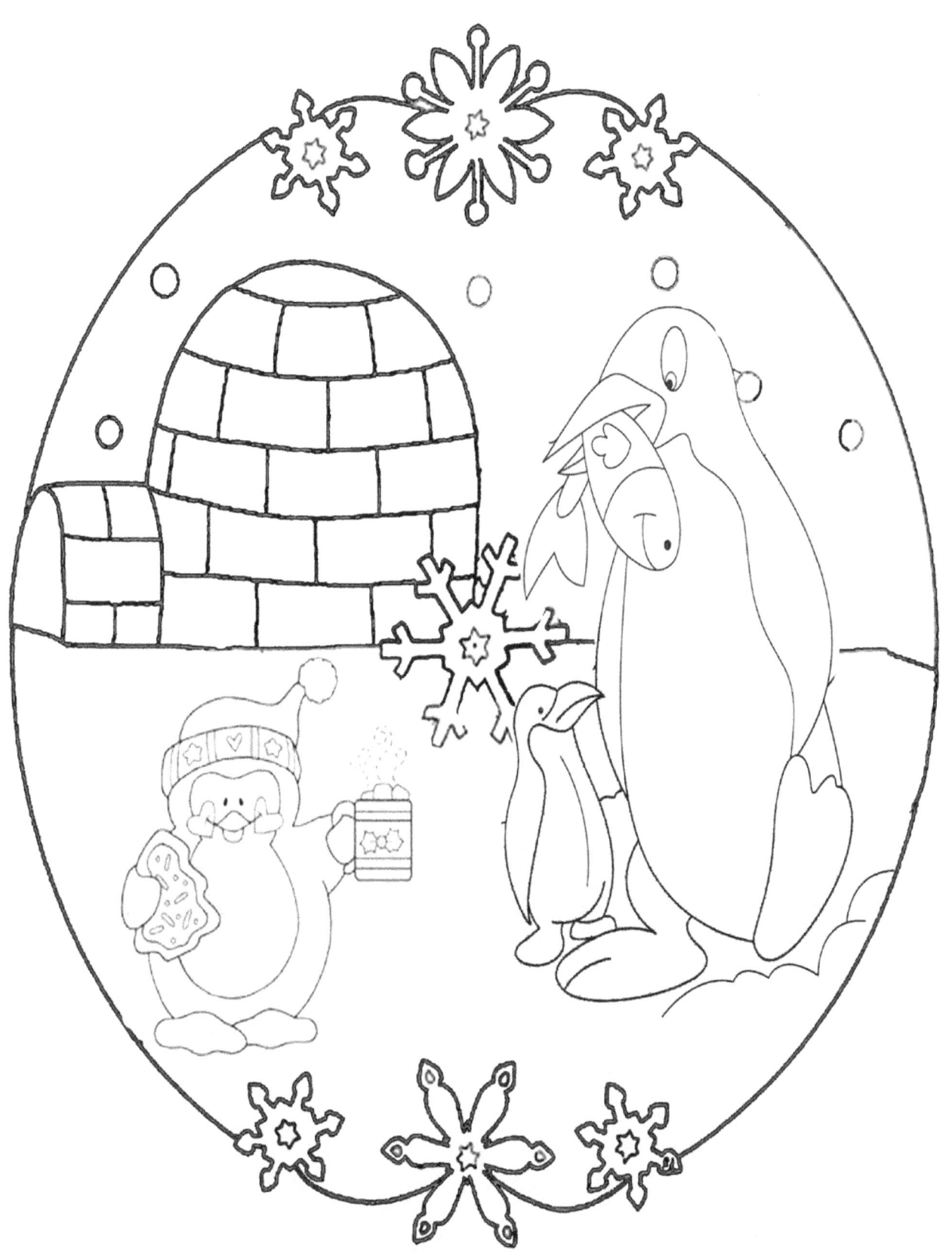

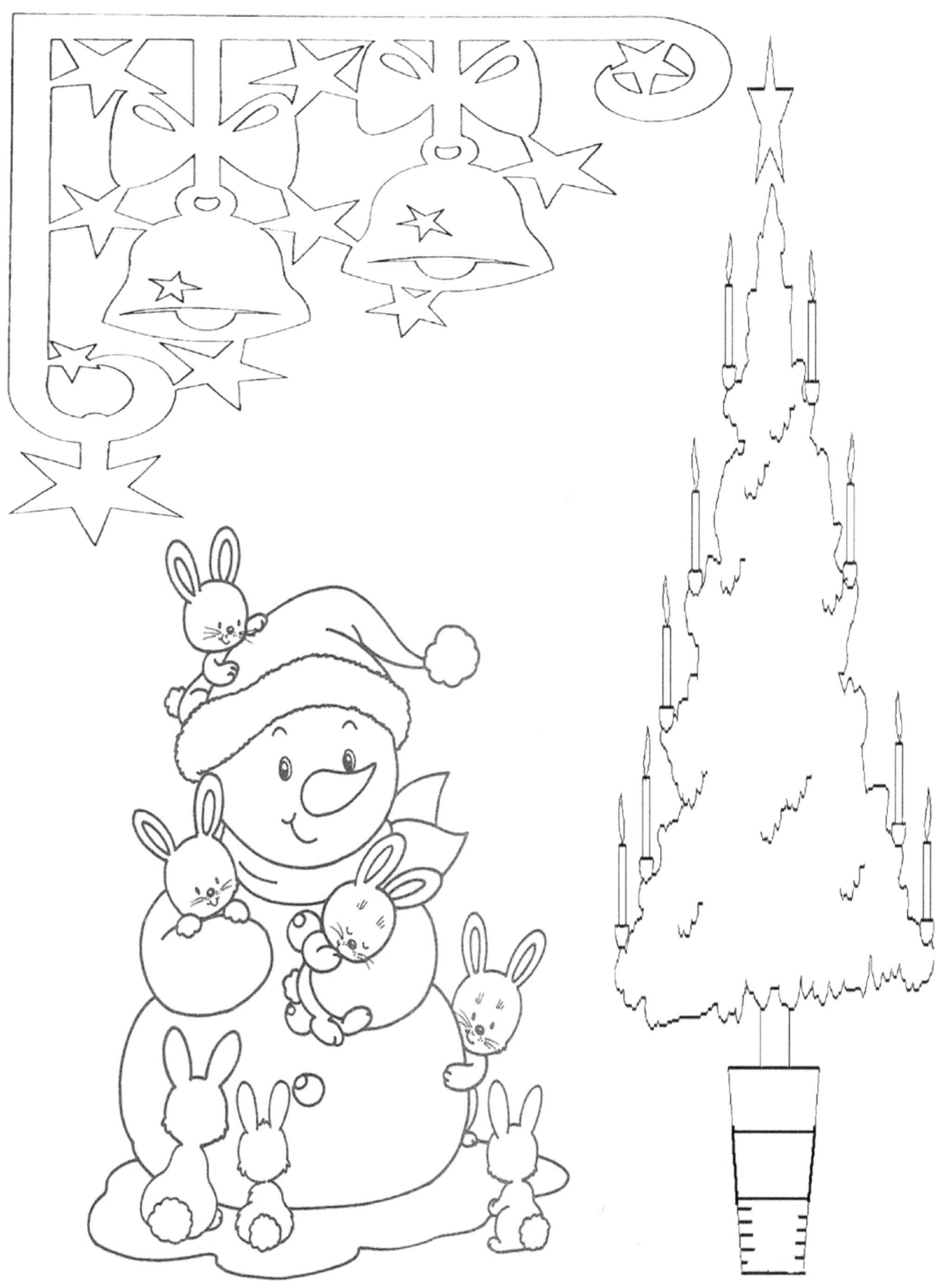

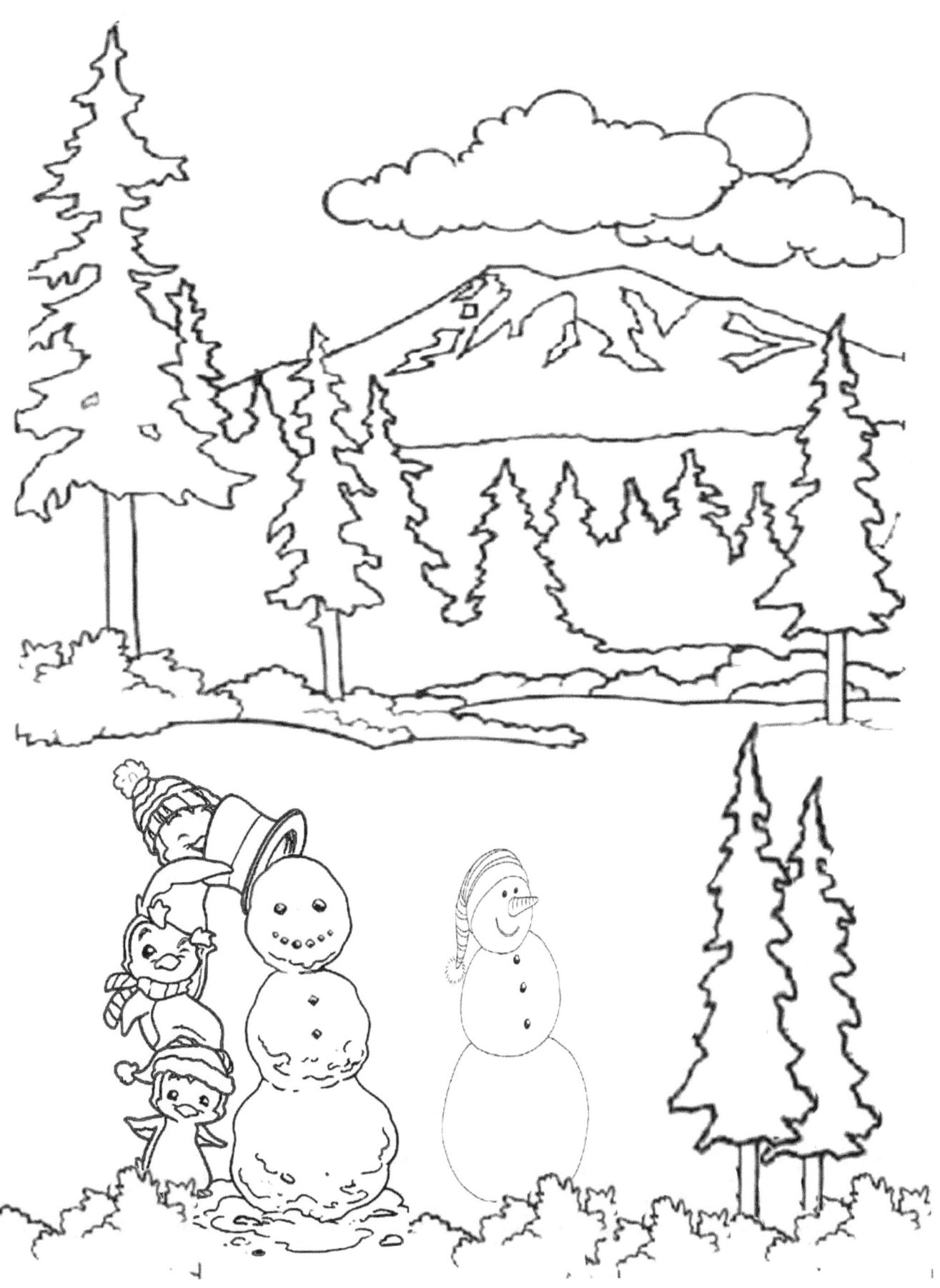

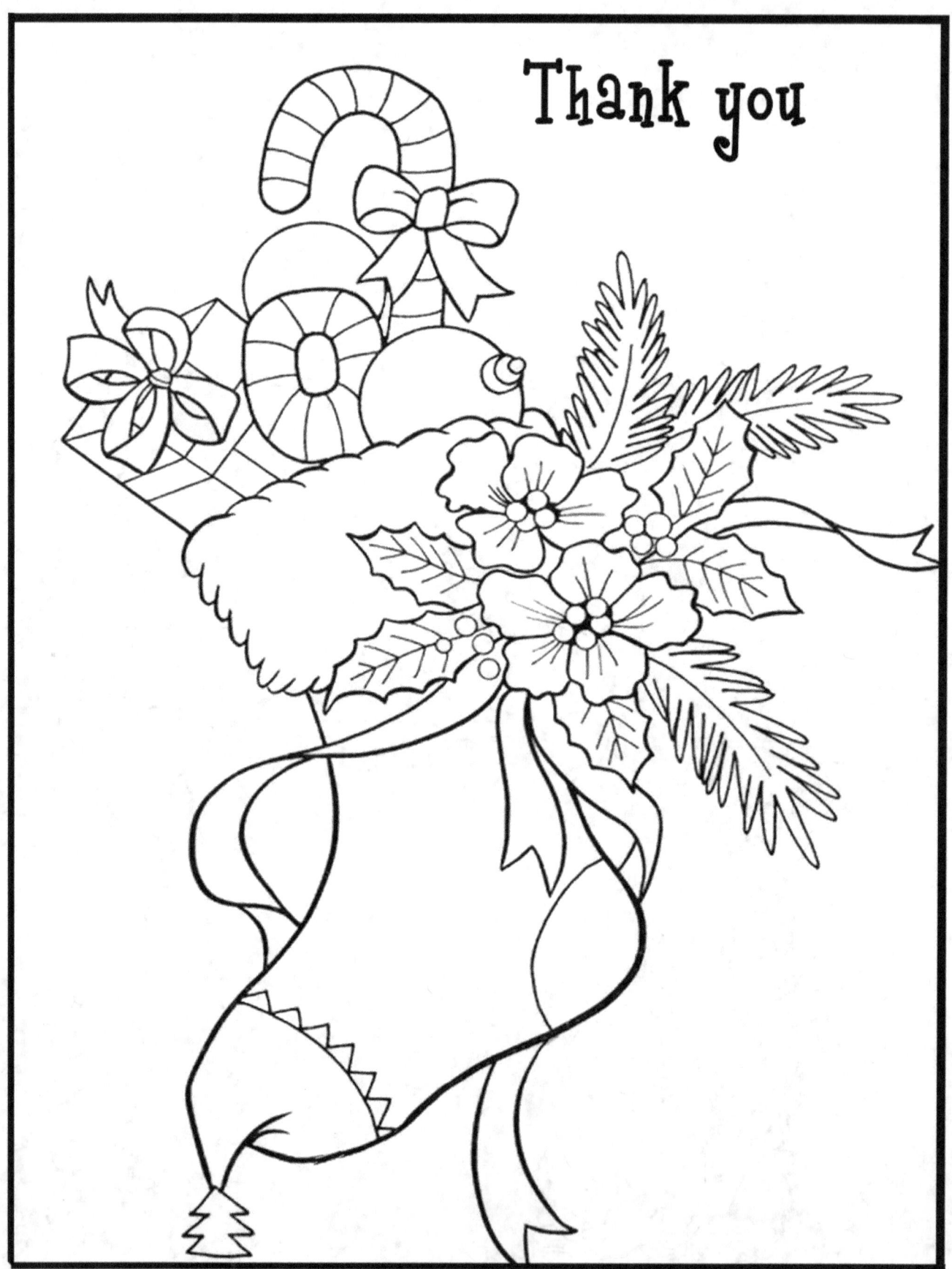

Thank you

www.ingramcontent.com/pod-product-compliance
Lightning Source LLC
Chambersburg PA
CBHW082118220526
45472CB00009B/2228